APPROACHING RETIREMENT

a Consumer Publication

edited by	Edith Rudinger
published by	Consumers' Association publishers of **Which?**
illustrations *and cover by*	Anna Kostal

Which? Books are commissioned and researched by
The Association for Consumer Research
and published by Consumers' Association,
14 Buckingham Street, London WC2N 6DS
and Hodder and Stoughton,
47 Bedford Square, London WC1B 3DP

ISBN 0 85202 349 9
and   0 340 40845 6

Photoset by Paston Press, Loddon, Norfolk
Printed and bound in Great Britain

APPROACHING RETIREMENT

a Consumer Publication

Consumers' Association
publishers of **Which?**
14 Buckingham Street
London WC2N 6DS

CONTENTS

FOREWORD

Retirement is an important event; it marks a new phase in life, and is a convenient time for taking stock and making certain decisions about the future. A big change in retirement will be in the amount of free time available, probably for the first time for over forty years, to organise your daily life without the restraints of set hours and a regular working routine. This may come as a shock to someone who has not thought how to spend his or her leisure; for others, it will be a release and the opportunity to do what they want, when they want to. A certain amount of planning will help you to enjoy a more content retirement: if you can remain actively involved in something – new, old or different – the continuing enjoyment of interests and activities can also contribute to health and wellbeing.

However, in spite of careful planning and enthusiastic anticipation, no one can predict what it will actually be like; do not feel disappointed if at first your retirement does not seem the happy release you anticipated. The sudden change, after years of working life, can be quite dramatic, and concern about the future may underlie the feeling of freedom: concern about getting older, becoming more dependent on others, having to manage on a progressively smaller income.

Finance is a potential source of worry for many people coming up to retirement. Some may be virtually as well-off as when they were working, but many will face a fall in income straightaway (or later on, if they are on a fixed pension). At this stage, far-reaching financial decisions may have to be taken, perhaps some – such as how to invest a lump sum – for the first time.

How you decide to organise your retirement so as to make the most of your new life is, of course, entirely up to you. This book aims to help you with some of the decisions that will face you.

THINKING ABOUT FINANCE

It is worth making financial plans well before you retire – five years ahead, if you can; even two ahead is better than nothing.

Try and make as detailed a forecast as possible of what your likely income will be when you stop work and what you will need to spend your money on, and how your spending pattern might change.

It is difficult to predict this, long before retirement, and particularly difficult to take account of inflation. However, you can – and should – revise your estimate regularly to keep it up to date.

income

Your income will almost certainly fall when you retire. Instead of a regular salary or wages you will receive an income from:

○ a basic retirement pension from the state
○ maybe a wife's pension
○ maybe an addition to your state pension, related to what you earned while employed
○ possibly an occupational pension from your employer, or a self-employed pension
○ the income from any savings and investments. But remember that its value may not keep pace with inflation; if you invest your money for maximum safety, it is generally sensible to make a pessimistic estimate of the income
○ other sources, such as any earnings from freelance part-time jobs.

spending

If you have never done any domestic budgeting, start with jotting down what you think your current spending pattern is. Then keep a careful detailed record for a few months – ideally for a whole year – of what you really spend (preferably day by day, or week by week). This will highlight exactly how you do spend your money now, and show how much you really need to spend on:

○ day to day items you buy regularly (food and drink, household goods, petrol, cigarettes)
○ regular lump sums, to pay bills which turn up regularly and at predictable intervals (the rates, mortgage, road tax, fuel bills)

○ leisure activities (books, cinema, pub, gardening)
○ irregular lump sums (money spent on major items such as holidays, new washing machine, redecorating the house)
○ unforeseeable expenditure (car repairs, a leaking roof).

The advantage of knowing where the money goes is that you can see at a glance where you could economise, if necessary, and what could be cut out altogether.

Around the time you retire, there will probably be a shift in your spending pattern. Some of this change relates to simply stopping work. For example, you will not have to pay fares to and from work, or for lunch out (on the other hand, you may find that you will need to spend more on food if you usually have lunch at a subsidised canteen). With more time available, you may plan to spend more on certain leisure activities which may cost money (such as playing bridge), but you may be able to take advantage of price concessions (for example 'first house' cinema, or theatre matinees). Bear this in mind when drawing up your budget.

Also try to take into account the effect of simply growing older. In your late sixties, you may want (or will need) to spend more than you do now, for example, on heating, on labour-saving appliances, on transport, including taxis. By looking several years ahead and allowing for this kind of age-related change in spending, you stand a better chance of being realistic when you work out your future budget, than if you assume you will spend your money in the same way as you did in your forties or fifties.

the effect of inflation
The value of money is likely to continue going down. Although certain investments and pensions are linked to inflation, salaries and wages are more likely to keep pace with inflation than do pensions, so the effect will be more noticeable. The rate of inflation cannot be predicted. Even if it is only 3%, for a sum to be worth £1,000 at to-day's prices, it would need to be £1,344 at the end of ten years, and £1,558 at the end of 15 years.

what will be different
Changes in your spending are likely to occur in these areas:

Family circumstances: your children will probably have left home and may be financially completely independent by the time you retire.

Regular financial commitments: you will probably be free of your mortgage by the time you retire. Payments into a personal pension scheme should also have ended.

Lifestyle: you may want to plan your holidays differently – travel in more comfort perhaps, or spend more on trips abroad. On the other hand, you may be able to save by being able to travel during the off-season and at reduced fares.

You may want to spend more time on, say, cooking and not rely on quickly prepared but expensive convenience food or frozen meals, but you may end up spending more money on special ingredients and on gas or electricity. There will be more time for 'entertaining' – inviting friends for drinks or a meal, for instance, which is enjoyable but also costs money. (If the invitations are reciprocated, that is also enjoyable, but not really money-saving.)

There will be more time for spending money on theatres, concerts, films – but you may be able to take advantage of cheaper tickets. More time for gardening may mean growing your own vegetables more successfully; the seeds cost very little, but the cost of fertilizers, insecticide, weedkillers, tools, all mount up.

Clothes: being retired does not mean that you have to go around looking dowdy, but there will be less need for formal clothing; you may find that you spend less money on smart clothes than when you were working. However, as people get older, they often need to spend more on warmer clothing.

Extra expenses: when you are older, you may no longer be prepared to walk in the pouring rain, so you may pay out more for bus rides (but there may well be fare concessions to take advantage of). You may also want, or will need, to get paid help with the housework.

A major cost, which cannot be postponed indefinitely after retirement, is having to replace household equipment as it, too, gets old. It is well worth buying new appliances while you are still earning if anything will need to be replaced before too long – refrigerator, washing machine, cooker. This may also be a good time to think about the car.

a gap between income and spending

If it looks as if you will need more money than you are going to have in retirement, the alternatives include:

○ spending less now on inessentials, so that you can save up for retirement while you still have a regular income
○ making additional voluntary contributions (AVCs) towards your pension
○ finding ways of increasing your income after retirement, by reorganising your investments to give income later
○ taking part-time work, if you can find it
○ moving to a smaller or less expensive home
○ getting rid of the car (which will bring a small lump sum and save running costs).

car
Amongst the advantages of having a car are the sheer convenience, not having to wait for public transport in wet and draughty conditions and not having to be exposed to colds and germs when travelling in crowded public vehicles. A car is invaluable when a necessary visit to the doctor or other medical help has to be made.

A car is, however, a major expense: insurance, vehicle licence tax, MoT test, are basic costs even if you drive only to the shopping centre once a week. To this has to be added the cost of petrol and oil, parking fees, servicing and repairs, depreciation (that is, how much less the car will be worth if and when you sell it).

If you drive less than about 4000 miles a year, it can be cheaper to hire a car rather than own one. This does not take into account the convenience of being able to step into your own car whenever you wish. And remember that if you hire a self-drive car, it has to be collected and returned to what may be an inconvenient point. Also, you will be driving only occasionally, and then an unfamiliar car.

If you are keeping a car, think about

○ changing to a car that use less petrol (both mpg and octane rating)
○ changing to a car in a low insurance group. (You may be able to reduce the insurance premium by taking what is known as an excess, that is being willing to pay part of any claim – say £50 – yourself.)
○ learning about car maintenance and doing some of it yourself which can save on garage bills
○ sharing some journeys and cost with a neighbour by using the car jointly or on set alternative dates (but that may lead to the end of a long friendship).

A couple who relies on a car for transport should make sure that both people can drive: it may be necessary in an emergency, and useful in everyday circumstances.

In a two-car family, giving up one of the two cars could save a lot of money. This makes economic sense, but be sure you think it through and talk it over first. In some cases, where a married couple sell one car, the husband continues to think of the car as his (and the wife can become a burden to her friends).

driving licence
The Driver and Vehicle Licensing Centre (DVLC) will normally send you a reminder to renew your licence about five weeks before it expires, so it is important to notify any change of address to DVLC Swansea SA6 7JL, quoting your driver number. Alternatively, you can get the renewal form D1 from any post office.

After 70, the licence can be renewed for three years, and then again for three years, and so on. On an application for a driving licence, details must be included of any physical or mental disabilities which may affect your ability to drive safely. If an entry on the form alerts the DVLC to the possible need for a medical examination, they send the form to their medical centre who may ask you to have a medical examination carried out by your own doctor and to provide a medical certificate, at your expense. It is possible that you will then be issued with a medically restricted licence. The medical restriction might be in terms of time, for example for only one year or two years where the disability is progressive, or restricted to a type of vehicle, for example Group A only for someone who has had an amputation.

Some insurance companies ask for a medical certificate every year after the age of 70 (or 73, or 75), before renewing the policy. The driver has to pay for the certificate. The fee for a medical certificate recommended by the British Medical Association is £24.50, but many doctors charge less in recognition of the applicant's limited means.

giving up the car?
Quite apart from the saving, you would no longer have to cope with the general hassle of driving, which will become more irritating as you get older. But do not do so lightly if you think that being without a car would leave you isolated.

WHERE TO LIVE

You may have had to live in a particular area because of your work; now may be your chance to get away. At 50-plus, start thinking about where you want to live when you stop work. List the advantages and disadvantages of staying where you are, to help clarify your thoughts about moving. If you decide that you will want to move, give yourself plenty of time to look round different areas.

When comparing the advantages of staying in the existing home with those of moving, you should try to think objectively about where you are living at present before making a decision, and answer some questions honestly:

○ Do you like your present home, and its environment? This will matter more when you have to spend the greater part of the day there. Being at home all day will make you more aware of the limitations and drawbacks of your environment. Do you know what it is like living there in the day time during the week? Neighbours may have children who have made a habit of playing outside your house after school every day or counted on being able to retrieve their ball from your garden. Perhaps your neighbour is a pianist who has practised during the weekdays for years – not a nuisance when you are not there, but could be intolerable when you are.

○ If your home large enough, light enough, warm enough, comfortable enough?

○ Do some of your family live nearby, or a particular friend? Do you get on with your neighbours? Do you like your doctor? Are you involved in many local activities? Can you get to the shops, post office, library, club, church easily?

Shops and public transport and other facilties may be too far away when the time comes to give up the car, or inconveniently located – for instance, on the other side of a busy road, or up a steep hill.

○ Have you got the garden just as you like it?

garden

Look particularly at the garden – is it large enough for your future gardening plans? Will it be too large to manage on your own in five, ten, twenty years' time? Can it be converted into an easy-care garden with minimal flower beds, no vegetable plots, no herbaceous border, more perennials?

Gardening involves quite hard physical work; bending and lifting get more difficult as people get older, particularly for someone suffering from arthritis (although light tools can make gardening easier).

Traditionally, gardening is high on the list of a retired person's activities, but if you dislike it or have always found it a chore, a large garden might be one factor in deciding to move.

If you sell your house, you may not want to leave mature plants, but you must have the purchaser's agreement to your removing plants you want to take with you.

should you move?

One reason for considering a move may be that the present home is, or is likely to become, too big. If your children have left and you are still working, you may think your three or four bedroomed house too big for just two of you, but a house of this size may be very convenient for two people who are at home all day. Space-taking hobbies are likely to expand with more leisure, and couples often find as they reach their fifties that a room of their own, where they can perhaps just write letters undisturbed, or leave the hobby ready to take up again later, is an excellent use of extra rooms. And if you have visiting family dropping in for an overnight stay from time to time, you will need an extra room, anyway.

For a house that is big and likely to become too expensive to run or maintain, you might – with great caution – consider sharing it with friends or members of the family. If you are thinking of taking lodgers, beware of the problems of getting rid of trouble-some tenants. The Consumer Publication *Renting and letting* gives advice on this.

You may think that your present house will eventually become too difficult to manage. It may have inconvenient stairs to climb, a lot of windows and floors to keep clean, a heating system that is not adequate or economical when you are at home all day.

Apart from the expense of a house and garden, and the worry about not having enough money for the necessary maintenance and repairs, when you get older you may feel exhausted and depressed by the physical struggle to keep a large old house cleaned, heated, and in good repair. Even a beloved garden may become a burden when everything grows faster than can be controlled.

On the other hand, maybe your accommodation now seems too small: a flat may have been quite adequate while you were at work, but when you are retired and spend much more time at home, a couple of rooms may not be enough.

But if you are thinking about moving to a larger place, consider carefully whether you have enough furniture, and enough money and energy to start a new type of home.

staying in the present home

If you decide not to move, it may be worth looking at your present home afresh, to see if the rooms could be more usefully arranged. The present arrangement of one bedroom, one dining room, one sitting room and one spare room could become two bedsitters, one study and a lounge with a large dining area.

Turning a spare bedroom into a workshop for d-i-y activities may be useful: the room will have electric sockets, possibly a water supply and will be a place to work in comfort without disrupting the rest of the household – and without having to clear up. Similarly, a small room where the sewing machine, and all that goes with it, can be left out permanently ready to use, and where a tailor's dummy will not be in anyone's way, may be a useful transformation from what used to be one of the children's bedrooms, now left intact for their occasional visits. If you transform all the spare rooms, however, try to make sure that you will still have room for visitors.

improving the home

Think about comfort and safety in the home and necessary repairs and possible improvements before you retire, while you have an income to cover any major expense. Now is the time for installing new equipment, and undertaking major decorations and maintenance.

If you have not had the wiring checked in the last ten years, have that done now by a competent electrician and, if necessary, have the house or flat rewired, and perhaps extra circuits put in. If you are having any electrical work done, it might be a good idea to have new sockets put in at a convenient place and height, where they are easy to reach.

Make sure that there is adequate lighting in every area of the house and especially on the stairs. If not, it should be possible to have two-way switches, so that you do not need to enter the house or cross the hallway or use the stairs in the dark.

Do not delay too long before dealing with house maintenance. The longer you wait before repairing a pipe or a leaking roof, the more consequential damage will occur and the more expensive the repair will be.

A kitchen could be made more convenient, and safer, with adequate work surfaces. A new cooker is an expensive piece of equipment, so if yours has become inefficient, it may be worth replacing it now with a new, split-level one with a separate hob, which saves having to bend down to lift out hot dishes.

Shelves and cupboards are often too high or too low, so give some thought to reorganising what you keep where, to avoid having to use steps too often. A strong pair of steps, preferably with a platform and handrail is useful – get in the habit of using them instead of doing a stretch-and-balance act on the kitchen stool.

The bathroom may also need attention. Consider having a shower installed which uses less hot water than a bath and is therefore more economical.

Remember to review the security arrangements of your home. It may be worth contracting your local police station, by telephone or by going there in person, to make an appointment for the local crime prevention officer to come to your home and carry out a security survey inside and outside the house. He should be able to give you detailed advice on how to make your home more secure. The police do not charge for advice from the crime prevention officer.

loans

A loan for home improvements will usually qualify for income tax relief up to a total loan (outstanding mortgage debt and the new loan) of £30,000. Check with the Inland Revenue if you are in doubt about your position.

If you have difficulty in getting a loan from your bank or building society, you may be able to get one from the local authority.

maturity loan

Write to the treasurer's department of your local authority and ask if you can be considered for a maturity loan for home improvement. You will have to show that a loan is necessary for the purpose, and that you cannot obtain the money from any other source.

The local authority will send a district valuer or local valuation officer to value your house. There may be a valuation fee (perhaps £20) which can be added to the amount of the loan.

You pay only the interest on a maturity loan; the capital has to be repaid after an agreed period, or when the house is sold, or the amount will be retrieved by the local authority when the house becomes part of your estate.

staying, but selling

You may no longer want the responsibility of being an owner-occupier even though you still want to live in your present home. It may be possible to sell the house to a housing association, thereby releasing capital and not having responsibility for major repairs. You would have to pay rent. The price paid by a housing association will not be high because they will be buying what amounts to tenanted property.

To find a housing association willing to do this in your area, ask the housing department of your local authority.

staying, but giving

The charity Help the Aged has a 'gifted house' scheme: you give the house to Help the Aged but continue to live there, rent free and with no responsibility for maintenance and repairs, upkeep of garden or payment of rates. If you later wish to, you can move to accommodation within the Help the Aged sheltered housing scheme.

A booklet giving details, *Gifted house plan*, is available from Help the Aged (Gifted Housing), The Court House, Ward Street, Guildford, Surrey GU1 4LH.

staying, with a home income plan

With this arrangement (also called a mortgage annuity scheme), you continue to own your home and on the security of it you get a loan (maximum £30,000) on which you pay interest which qualifies for tax relief. With the amount of the loan, the lending company buys you an annuity which pays you an income for the rest of your life. The interest payments you have to make are deducted from the annuity income you receive; most home income plans involve payment of an administration fee to the company. The loan has to be repaid if you sell the home during your lifetime, or out of your estate after your death.

Where the scheme involves a variable interest, your income will go down if the interest rate is raised; where it is a fixed-interest loan, you may be missing out on getting more income if interest rates generally go down.

Most companies which operate home income plans do not accept anyone under the age of 70 (or, in the case of a married couple, with a combined age of 150).

If you are receiving a means-tested social security benefit such as housing benefit or supplementary pension, the income from a home income plan may affect your entitlement: the extra income would be deducted from the pension entitlement, or might push you above the benefit's income threshold.

staying, with a home reversion scheme

You continue to live in your home but sell your interest in it, or a proportion of it, to a financial institution (a reversion company) for a one-off lump sum or an annuity income. The cash sum from the sale will rarely be more than 50 per cent of the value of the house and may be 20 per cent or even less, and an administration fee of about $1\frac{1}{2}$ per cent of the value of the house has usually to be paid for arranging the sale.

Some reversionary schemes buy your home and give you an income which rises in line with the value of all the homes in the scheme.

The occupant (you) remains in the house rent-free or for a nominal monthly sum, but remains responsible for repairs, maintenance and the rates.

Before you commit yourself to such a scheme, make sure that there are no circumstances in which you could be forced to leave, and also find out how any annuity you get from the home reversion scheme would be affected if you decide that you want to move away in the future.

Such a scheme differs from the others described above in that it involves selling your home, as against raising a loan on it. You would be wise to seek independent financial advice before you go ahead.

Moving

If you decide that you need a different house, and will want to move, plan as far ahead as you can and do some thinking and researching.

when?

You may feel that you would like to live in your new home for a couple of years before you retire, so as to get to know the people and places as a 'working person' rather than a 'retired' one.

However, if you decide to put off a move for, say, two years, you will have the opportunity to find out more about yourself and the sort of life you lead when retired, and therefore to have more idea of the sort of district and home that will suit you.

If you move immediately on retirement, you start your new life in new surroundings. But it may be more convenient to house-hunt and move when you have more free time for the actual business of putting your present house or flat on the market, finding and buying a new one, and the whole process of sorting out, getting rid of the accumulated junk of years, packing, and all the worry that goes with a move – even if it is only to a new home three streets away.

On a very practical point, it is easier to move in the spring or summer than in mid-winter. The book *Which? way to buy, sell and move house* deals with the whole subject in great detail.

council tenants

Generally it is difficult for somebody who owns a house to get on the local authority list for a council tenancy, but if your house is large and would be suitable for conversion, you may be able to sell it to the council in exchange for a council flat or bungalow.

An existing council tenant who wants to give up a large family size house which has become too big may be able to get it exchanged for more suitable accommodation such as a bungalow or flat.

Some local authorities keep an exchange list of tenants who want to move into council accommodation elsewhere within their area; or two tenants may be able to arrange an exchange independently. It is not easy to move into a different local authority; few authorities keep lists of council tenants who wish to move to a neighbouring authority. It is similarly difficult to arrange a move to a local authority farther away, but a nationwide private exchange scheme for council tenants called Locatex Bureau whose address is PO Box 1, March, Cambridgeshire PE15 8HJ, can match council tenants who wish to offer or exchange their tenancy with one in another part of the country. Locatex charges a small fee, usually around £7.

The Tenants Exchange Scheme has been introduced by the government to help public sector tenants in England, Scotland and Wales who want to exchange homes with a tenant in another council's area. The scheme is also available to tenants wanting to move to or from (but not within) Northern Ireland. Details and a registration form, with notes on how to complete it, can be obtained from the Tenants Exchange Scheme, PO Box 170, London SW1P 3PX and from your local authority housing department.

The National Mobility Scheme is a voluntary scheme agreed between most housing authorities in the UK to help tenants move to a different area if they have a pressing need to move, such as to be near an elderly relative who needs support. For more details, and a nomination for a move under the scheme, go to your own housing authority or housing association.

A booklet *Wanting to Move?* (no. 12 in the Department of the Environment's series of housing booklets) is available from local councils and citizens advice bureaux. It gives advice to people wanting to rent (including privately) or buy in a new area.

some financial considerations

The points you should consider are:

○ the size and value of your home now
○ the size and value of the home you will need when you retire
○ what you can buy elsewhere with the proceeds of selling the present home
○ the income from investing any surplus lump sum, if what you get from selling is more than you need for buying
○ the cost of moving
○ the saving you could make in running costs by moving to a smaller house (rates, heating, maintenance); conversely, the increase if you move to a larger one
○ the savings you may be able to make by living in a cheaper area (and vice versa).

If you think that it will make sense to move, get some idea of the value of your present home and also what you might have to pay for the kind of house or flat you want. Then make some estimate of the cost of moving (which may be up to 10 per cent or so of the value of your new house). If you need or want more money, you can 'trade down', that is buy cheaper than the house you are selling (smaller, or in a less expensive area) and get a lump sum. You can then work out how much will be left for you to invest as a result of your move to give you more income, if you are worried that your income will be too low when you retire.

If you decide to move, one advantage of doing so straightaway is that there may be a lump sum from your pension to spend on a house (which may be vital if you have been living in rented accommodation and are an elderly first-time-buyer). A person who is approaching retirement age, or has passed it, may not be able to get a mortgage from a building society and would have to find some other lender. Also, an older borrower would probably have to provide additional security and may have to pay higher interest rates for a short-term loan.

how often?
It is worth considering whether it is better to make only one move to a house or flat which will be suitable for the remainder of your life, or whether it is advisable to plan for two phases – the active and less active – and risk the unsettling effect of a second move at a later time when it may be less easy to adjust.

Difficult though it may be, try to anticipate your needs and attitudes ten, or even twenty, years from now. If there are two of you, consider also what kind of home would be suitable for your widow/widower living there alone.

Ideally, you will want a flat, bungalow or easily maintained house you like, in an area where you will feel safe, in a situation that will sustain you as you become older and less mobile, preferably near family or friends, with shops and transport facilities near, and which will not become too expensive to live in and maintain.

where?

Many people think of retiring to the country or to the seaside. However, at a seaside resort, property may cost more than it does where you now live (and food and services may be more expensive, too). Remember that it is very different living permanently in the middle of the country, or all the year round in a seaside resort, compared with spending a happy two-week holiday there in the height of summer. Apart from walks in the country and by the sea, will other activities be available to you?

assessing the location

It is a good idea to go and stay in the area you have in mind, wherever it may be, at different times of the year. Try and make an assessment of the area and what living there would entail, starting with the shopping.

○ How good is the shopping? Is most of what you need, or are likely to want, available in the locality? Are things more expensive than you have been used to?

You should try to do a genuine comparison of your 'shopping basket' cost for a week. That does not mean that you have to buy all the items, but try to go to the various local shops (not just chain supermarkets which probably charge the same wherever they are located), with paper and pencil and note down the prices. Do this for all that you would need to pay for – not just groceries but also the prices of services such as shoe repairs, and dry cleaners, and cinemas, and afternoon tea in a local tea shop.

○ Is it possible to walk to shops, post office, library, a social centre? Are there facilities for you to carry on with a hobby, an interest, an evening course?

○ What is public transport like; would you have to depend on the car?

○ Does getting about locally mean having to go up and down a hill?

○ How easy would it be to visit friends and relatives, and for them to come to you?

o Would you be happy, or at least content, to go on living in the area if your spouse or companion died, or would you want to move again?
o What would happen in times of illness?
o What is the situation about doctors or a health centre and ancillary services, such as chiropody?

If you are thinking of moving to an area that is popular with retired people, general practitioners are likely to have a high proportion of elderly patients on their lists, and may find it difficult to accept new ones.

In an area with a predominantly ageing population, there may be a strain on the welfare services and more people needing help than there are people able to give it. Try to find out, for instance, the length of waiting time for a chiropody appointment or an appointment at a hearing aid clinic.

Only if you decide you like the area in general and have checked that it is likely to be suitable for you, should you start looking for a particular flat or house.

MOVING ABROAD

You may decide that you would like to live abroad after retirement, perhaps because you have visited a country on holiday and like the way of life there, or because you would like to escape to a warmer, sunnier climate. However, consider all the aspects and implications even more carefully than if you were intending to move to a new area in the UK.

The first decision is where to live, and then to discover, as far as possible, what it is like to live there. It might be worth spending a fair bit of time there before you retire, to explore the area to find out what living there really entails – as against being on holiday. Visit the area at different times of the year, not only during the holiday season or the off-peak season, in either of which the atmosphere and the facilities may be atypical.

practical aspects

Not speaking the language of a country would be a great barrier, so if you do not know it yet, make sure that you will be able to learn it. Even so, there is a risk of being isolated, or dependent on an expatriate group. You will probably see less of your family, certainly as far as casual visits are concerned (though they, and others, may want to spend their holidays with you there). If you go and visit them, the fares may be high.

You may think that eventually, when you are very old, you will prefer to be back in Britain and that you should therefore buy a bungalow in Bognor. The tax implications of this are complex. Briefly, if you have accommodation available for your use in the UK, you are regarded as resident for any year in which you visit the UK, and ordinarily resident if you come here most years. The Inland Revenue leaflet IR 20 (Residents and Non-residents Liability to Tax in the UK) gives details.

Living abroad will involve a completely different lifestyle and therefore different attitude of mind; you should be aware of this before committing yourself to life in another country.

Remember that services may be very different from those in the UK, such as no doorstep delivery of milk. It may be difficult, or very expensive, to obtain such everyday items as British newspapers. If possible, talk to other British people living in the area and find out their views, and go shopping to see what is readily available, at what prices. Food may be cheap, health care and transport may be expensive, for example. Find out what the public transport system is like – expensive or cheap, reliable or unreliable, frequent or infrequent?

formal aspects

It is important to check pension arrangements in the country where you wish to live. Your state pension can be paid to you, free of UK taxes, in most parts of the world, but you would have to check with your local social security office whether subsequent increases in the pension can be received. Countries where increases are payable at present include all the EEC countries, Austria, Bermuda, Cyprus, Finland, Gibraltar, Guernsey, Iceland, Israel, Jamaica, Jersey, Malta, Mauritius, Sark, Switzerland, Turkey, USA, Yugoslavia; notable exceptions include Canada and Australia. If you do not get the increase while you are abroad, you will get the higher rate of pension if you return or visit the UK. The lower rate will again be paid when you leave if your stay in the UK was only temporary.

Health facilities are most impotant. See if a health service exists and whether you would be eligible to use it (and, if so, under what conditions). Local health insurance may be available; check whether your British private health insurance, if you have this, covers residence in the country you want to live in. Try to find out what the standard of medical care is and what, if any, ancillary services there are for the elderly.

It is also vital to investigate local tax regulations; to know whether you need to become a registered resident of the country and what the conditions of doing so are; to make sure you understand your own legal position as a foreign resident. You may need to seek professional advice on these points; in the first place, contact the embassy of the country where you intend to live, to ask specific questions.

check list:

○ health services, availability of drugs;
○ resident's permit: how, when, for how long, restrictions, cost;
○ work permit, giving (unofficial?) english lessons;
○ tax abroad – income tax, dual taxation, local taxes (for residents/ foreigners);

○ tax situation in UK while living abroad, earning, non-earning, short return visits to UK, double taxation relief arrangements;
○ what happens when there is a change in exchange control regulations: effects on pension payments, effects on dividends, banking arrangements;
○ professional advice abroad;
○ social security and medical care agreements: see the DHSS leaflets for the relevant country, in the SA series, and (for EEC countries) SA.29 *Your social security and pension rights in the EC.*

PENSIONS

For many people, their main income in retirement will be a
pension: from the state and perhaps from an employer's scheme
(an occupational pension) or one from a personal pension plan
paid for from self-employed earnings or when not a member of an
employer's scheme.

a pension from the state

You can receive a state pension when you reach the official pensionable age of 65 (for men) or 60 (for women) and retire from regular work. You will generally count as 'retired' for pension purposes if

○ you do not do any paid work at all, or
○ you do not work for more than 12 hours a week, or
○ you work only occasionally, or
○ you do not normally earn more than £75 a week.

When you reach the age of 70 (for men) or 65 (for women), you will be paid your state pension even if you have still not officially retired.

who is eligible?

How much pension you will get from the state when you come to retire (or whether any at all) depends on the contributions you will have made to the national insurance scheme throughout your working life, as an employee or when self-employed, or by contributing voluntarily.

employees
National insurance contributions have to be paid by employed people who earn above a certain minimum and by people who are self-employed. Employers also pay contributions based on their employees' wages.

An employee earning more than what is called the 'lower earnings limit' pays class 1 contributions which are a percentage of total weekly earnings up to an 'upper earnings limit'. These limits change each year: for 1986/87, they were £38 and £285 a week; from April 1987, they go up to £39 and £295 respectively. Between the lower earnings and upper earnings limits, the percentage rate of contributions increases on a set scale.

self-employed

A self-employed person pays a class 2 contribution which is a flat-rate figure: £3.75 a week for 1986/87; from April 1987, £3.85.

If you were employed and also self-employed for any period during any year and therefore paid class 2 as well as class 1 contributions, each of the class 2 contributions counts as if it were a class 1 contribution at the lower earnings level and therefore gains you some additional pension.

voluntary

Class 3 contributions, which can be paid voluntarily by anyone wanting to maintain his or her national insurance contribution record during non-earning periods when not being credited with contributions, for example while studying, or out of the country. Class 3 contributions are a flat-rate figure: currently, £3.65 a week, increasing to £3.75 from April 1987.

DHSS records

Each person's national insurance record is kept by the Department of Health and Social Security (DHSS). At any time before you reach pensionable age, you can ask the local DHSS office how your record stands at that particular date. If you give your full name, date of birth and national insurance number, they will work out for you what percentage of the basic state pension your present record will quality you for – 100% or 90% or 85%, or whatever. What this will mean in exact amounts will depend on the current rate of pension being paid when you retire and on your keeping up your national insurance record in the intervening years.

The basic rate of pension is increased regularly in line with inflation so the present figure is a guide to what you will be getting in terms of today's buying power.

The DHSS leaflet NP32 *Your retirement pension* gives full details of contribution requirements and the types of pension. Leaflet NI 196 lists the current rates, and there is also a general leaflet FB6 *Retiring? your pension and other benefits*. All DHSS leaflets are free and are available at social security offices, also some post offices, citizens advice bureaux and, for reference, local libraries.

what pension you qualify for

Under the present state pension scheme, which started in April 1978, a retirement pension consists of

○ a basic pension

This is paid at a flat rate, regardless of what you have been earning.

○ an earnings-related pension

This is an additional component, based on earnings between the lower and higher earnings limits throughout the years from April 1978. An employee who is a member of an employer's pension scheme that is contracted out of the state scheme does not get this additional component; instead, the employer's scheme undertakes to pay a broadly equivalent amount.

○ a graduated pension

Someone who paid graduated national insurance contributions on a set band of earnings during the years 1961 to 1975 will get a small extra amount added to the basic pension, according to the number of 'units' accumulated.

basic pension

Whichever 'class' of national insurance contributions you have been paying, or if you mixed them in any one year, all count towards your record to qualify you for a basic pension. But employed married women who chose to pay a reduced rate of class 1 contributions cannot claim a pension on the basis of those contributions. They are dependent on their husband's contribution record for a pension.

contributions: how many and for how long
To qualify for the basic pension, you will have to pass two contribution 'tests'. The first is that you must have paid or been credited with a minimum number of national insurance contributions in each tax year during your working life.

Any time during which your earnings as an employee were below the lower earnings level set for that year will show as a gap in your contribution record, because no contributions will have been deducted from your pay under that level.

In certain circumstances when you were not earning, you will have been credited with national insurance contributions without having to make any payments. This will have happened, for example, when you were drawing unemployment benefit, or sickness or invalidity benefit, and while a woman was getting maternity allowance.

The second test is that you must have paid or been credited with contributions for a given number of tax years during your working life.

You will need to have contributed for nearly a quarter of the years in your working life in order to get any basic pension at all and for approximately nine out of ten in order to get the full pension.

There have been various changes, particularly in the bases for calculating how much pension is paid, since the present national insurance scheme started in 1948. People of different age groups have to qualify in different ways, according to when they started to be in the system.

A crucial date is 5 July 1948.

For anyone who was over 16 on 5 July 1948 (therefore now aged 55 or more) who was not at that time contributing to a pension under any previous, non-compulsory, state scheme, the period during which you will be expected to have contributed will start from 6 April 1948 – even if at that time you were not working. This period is known as your 'working life'.

For anyone over the age of 16 in 1948 who was already contributing to the then state pension scheme, the period during which you will be expected to have contributed starts from the beginning of the tax year in which you started paying into the scheme or, if there was a break in employment, last started contributing.

So, someone's retiring in 1987 will need to have had a working life of 39 years to get the maximum pension due to him or her; 35 years' contributions would be enough because there is some leeway.

qualifying years and working life
The concept of 'qualifying' years was introduced in April 1975. It is based on the earnings threshold for paying class 1 contributions.

A working year counts as qualifying if in it you have paid, or were credited with, contributions on a specified multiple of the lower earnings limit relevant for that year:

○ between 6 April 1975 and 5 April 1978
  50 times the lower earnings limit for the year
○ from 6 April 1978
  52 times the lower earnings limit for the year.

You will not get any pension at all unless

○ before 6 April 1975, you paid 50 flat-rate contributions
○ from 6 April 1975, you paid (rather than being credited with) enough contributions in any one tax year for that year to be a qualifying year.

(A year of working life or a year of national insurance contributions refers to a tax year – the 12 months from 6 April to the following 5 April.)

Working life is an official definition. It means the tax years from the year in which you reached the age of 16 to the tax year ending before the year in which you reach pensionable age. So, a man's working life is generally 49 years and a woman's 44 years. If you were born before 5 July 1932, the length of your working life may be slightly shorter because the current national insurance scheme started when you were already over 16 years old.

The number of qualifying years normally needed is:

length of working life	*number of qualifying years needed*
10 years or less	length of working life minus 1
11–20 years	length of working life minus 2
21–30 years	length of working life minus 3
31–40 years	length of working life minus 4
41 years or more	length of working life minus 5

missed contributions

If you are now 50-plus and had an unsettled earlier working life, or in the last few years your earnings as an employee were below the level for making class 1 national insurance contributions, there are likely to be gaps or inadequacies in your national insurance record. You should look back and try to work out when and for how long you missed out on paying, and ask the DHSS (through your local social security office) how much you would need to make up.

voluntary payments

Missed contributions can be made up by paying class 3 contributions any time up to the end of the 6th year after the year in which you had missed making contributions. (Before April 1985, there was a two-year limit on making up missed contributions.)

DHSS leaflet NI 48 *Unpaid and late paid contributions* gives details of when you can make back payment of contributions and leaflet NI 42 explains about voluntary contributions.

home responsibilities protection

If in any tax year since 1978, you were at home caring for an elderly or sick relative who was receiving attendance allowance or you were receiving supplementary benefit or invalid care allowance during that time, your right to a basic state pension may have been protected. This 'home responsibilities protection' reduces the number of years' contributions you would otherwise need in order to qualify for a full basic pension. (But the minimum that period can be reduced to is 20 years, or half the number of years that would be required in your case, whichever is less.) When the time comes to claim your pension, those years will automatically be deducted from the number required to qualify you for the basic pension.

This home responsibilities protection applies also to a parent who is not working and is at home looking after a child or children under the age of 16, for whom the parent receives child benefit. Child benefit is normally paid to the mother, so if it is the father who is staying at home to care for the children, the child benefit must be signed over to him by the mother in order to ensure that he will get this protection for his pension.

Home responsibilities protection is accorded automatically by the DHSS to anyone whose circumstances qualify him or her (a married women who opted to pay reduced rate stamps on giving up work does not quality).

Leaflet NP27 *Looking after someone at home: how to protect your pension* gives full details.

married woman

A woman who gives up paid work when she married can stop paying national insurance contributions. Unless she can qualify on her own previous national insurance record, she will then be dependent on her husband's national insurance record to provide her retirement pension. She will not get this until he retires and she is herself over 60.

A married man's national insurance contributions entitle him to a basic pension for his wife as well as for himself. If she is under 60 when he retires and is not earning more than a specified amount, he gets an addition to his pension for her as a dependant. Once she is over 60 and counts as retired, she receives a pension of about 60 per cent of her husband's basic pension (whether reduced or full). There is no corresponding entitlement for a married woman to claim a dependant's pension for her husband based on contributions she has made.

When she is 60, a wife whose pension is based on her husband's national insurance record gets the pension paid to her separately.

Before that age, any allowance for her comes within her husband's pension payment.

There used to be an option until 1978 for a woman who married and continued in paid employment to pay contributions at a reduced rate, which does not qualify her for a retirement pension. This option is no longer offered, but any married woman who opted to pay at the lower rate and continued to work could go on paying the reduced rate and be dependent on her husband's national insurance contributions for her state pension.

her own contribution record

A married woman who has gone on paying full-rate class 1 contributions will be eligible for a pension in her own right, as if she were a single person, provided she has the appropriate number of qualifying years in her working life. The working years do not necessarily have to be consecutive but can be cumulative, so that other years can be added on during which contributions were credited – for example, when receiving invalidity benefit.

A woman who has decided to stop working when she is, say, 56 years old should find out from the DHSS whether topping up her existing record by paying voluntary (class 3) contributions for the remaining few years would get her a better pension at 60. If she is less than 5 years younger than her husband and will therefore reach retirement age first, she may be able to draw her own pension in the intervening years to his retirement. And if her pension in her own right is greater than the pension she would get on her husband's record when he reaches retirement age, she will continue get the higher amount.

A woman who marries relatively late in life, or for a second time, and gives up paid work, should find out from the DHSS before deciding whether or not to make further national insurance contributions whether her own national insurance record or her husband's is likely to produce the higher amount of pension. If some crucial contributions have been missed, she can then make them up by class 3 contributions, provided she does so before the end of the sixth year after the gap.

after divorce or death of spouse

A widow or a divorced woman can get a pension based on her late or ex-husband's national insurance record. This will be used either wholly for her basic pension or to supplement her own contribution record in order to gain a higher rate of pension.

A widower or divorced man, too, can substitute his late or ex-wife's national insurance record for all his working years while they were married up to the end of the tax year in which she died or they were divorced, if her record will provide a better basic pension than his own.

DHSS leaflet NP 32A explains about your retirement pension if you are widowed or divorced.

When a divorced couple have lost all contact with each other, the DHSS should be able to trace the relevant contribution record; ask your local social security office, giving as many details as you can of your divorced spouse.

When a woman's husband dies after the age of 65 and the widow is over sixty then, her retirement pension will be changed to the rate for a widow; in addition, she will get half any graduated pension he had been entitled to, and any extra pension he had earned by deferring his retirement.

earnings-related pension

In addition to the basic flat-rate pension, anyone who has been earning as an employee more than the statutory lower earnings limit for each year since 6 April 1978 will get an addition to the basic pension, relating to those earnings. The exception is that employees who belong to an employer's pension scheme which has contracted out of this part of the state scheme do not get this earnings-related addition because their employer's scheme will have had to guarantee to provide at least as much; their national insurance contributions will have been at a lower rate accordingly.

People whose earnings come from self-employment do not get an earnings-related addition: their class 2 national insurance contributions qualify them only for the basic state pension.

The state earnings-related pension (nowadays referred to as SERPS) depends on the level of your earnings on which you will have been paying class 1 contributions over the years. Even if you do not qualify for the basic pension because of insufficient national insurance contributions during your working life, you may get some earnings-related pension.

A married woman who has been paying full national insurance contributions will get any additional pension based on her earnings paid to her in her own right, even if she is relying for her basic pension on her husband's contribution record.

What you will get as an additional pension will depend on

○ how many tax years you have worked between 6 April 1978 and the 5 April immediately before you reach pensionable age
○ your earnings during those years
○ the increase in average earnings in the country as a whole during those years (measured by an index published by the Department of Employment).

The additional pension you will get each week is the sum of 1/80th of each of the years' earnings, revalued in line with the Department of Employment's index, divided by 52. This is a complicated calculation. An example is given in the DHSS leaflet NP32, and your local social security office should be able to tell you how much additional pension you yourself will qualify for.

if contracted out
If your employer's pension scheme is one which is contracted out of the state earnings-related scheme, you will not get the additional state pension (and will have been paying national insurance contributions at a proportionately lower rate while a member of that employer's scheme). An occupational pension scheme established before November 1986 had, in order to be allowed to contract out of the state scheme, to guarantee to provide 'requisite benefits' to those provided by the state scheme. Since that date, the criteria have been relaxed, and an employer can contract his scheme out of the state scheme provided he undertakes to pay a minimum contribution into his employees' scheme, rather than

undertaking to pay out a minimum amount, as previously established schemes have to do. If your employer's scheme is one contracted-out under the previous regulations, the guaranteed minimum part of your earnings-related pension will be kept topped up by the state fund once you start to get it, so that it remains in line with any general increases in prices.

graduated pension

If you were employed between April 1961 and April 1975 and paid graduated contributions into the then state pension scheme, related to your earnings, you will get extra pension per week from those contributions.

What you get consists of so-many pence per 'unit' of graduated contributions: for a man, the unit is £7.50, for a woman £9. Someone retiring in 1987/88 will get 5.17p per unit (the unit payment is increased each year in line with inflation). When the graduated scheme ended in 1975, everyone who had contributed was sent a statement of how much they had paid in and how many units they had thereby accumulated. By multiplying the number of units to your credit by the current per-unit payment, you can work out how much you will get by way of graduated pension.

Getting a graduated pension does not depend on qualifying for a basic pension. A married woman who has earned her own graduated pension can claim this when she reaches 60 and retires even if she is then not getting the basic pension – for instance, because she is relying on her husband's contribution record for this and he has not yet retired. A widow(er) can inherit half the late spouse's graduated pension entitlement to add to her own or his own, irrespective of her or his own eligibility; but the amount of graduated pension the widow(er) receives in all must not be more than the maximum a single person would get.

retiring early, retiring later

If you want or have to give up paid work before you reach state pension age, you cannot draw any part of your state pension until you reach that age. This applies even if your early retirement is brought about by ill health (but you can claim sickness benefit or invalidity benefit meanwhile).

If you do decide to retire before pensionable age, you should ask your local social security office to check whether your national insurance record up to the date you plan to retire is sufficient to provide a full basic pension when you reach the qualifying age. If not, find out whether it would be worth making voluntary (class 3) contributions during the intervening months or years to make your record as complete as possible. Contributions could be made up to the end of the tax year beore the one which includes your qualifying birthday (65th for a man, 60th for a woman).

unemployed before retirement

A man who becomes unemployed between the ages of 60 and 65 is credited with national insurance contributions, even if he is not drawing unemployment benefit, for any time during the period from the start of the tax year before his 60th birthday to the end of the one before his 65th birthday. This means that his retirement pension when he reaches the age of 65 will be calculated as if he had been making contributions during those years.

A man who stops working between the age of 60 and 65 does not need to sign on for employment or claim unemployment benefit (though he can claim, if he wants to and is eligible) in order to get credited.

A woman under 60, however, does not get credits during her 'last' five years in a similar way, nor does a man until he is 60 years old. Many people nowadays have to retire at 55 or, in any case, under 60 and should – if necessary – make up their contribution record by paying voluntary contributions.

retiring later

The age at which you retire, can make a difference to the amount of pension you will get from the state.

If you decide not to retire at the state pensionable age, you have to tell the DHSS on the form that will be sent to you a few months prior to your birthday, which asks "Do you intend to retire?". Putting the answer "No", means that payment of your state pension will be postponed until either you do retire or you reach the age of 65 (woman) or 70 (man), when you will get the state pension (basic plus earnings-related) that you have earned up to that date.

You should get your right to a pension established at your pensionable age; the DHSS can tell you what is payable to you then, including any additional components (earnings-related or graduated).

An addition will be made to your eventual pension for every six days (i.e. each week excluding sunday) after the first 7 weeks of your deferred retirement. The increase is one-seventh of a penny for every £ of the pension you qualified for on your qualifying birthday (1p for every 7 weeks you put off retirement).

If you are continuing with your full-time job or are changing to a part-time or freelance job for at least the first years after your official retirement age, you might as well forgo the state pension during that time, so as to gain the increase. You do not get the increase for any period during postponed retirement when you are receiving any national insurance benefit.

If you go on earning after pensionable age, you do not have to pay national insurance contributions (but whoever is employing you will have to pay his or her statutory percentage of your pay).

If, after you have retired, you take up well-paid work again, you can 'cancel' your retirement, by notifying the DHSS, and your pension will be held for you and increased in the same way as an initially deferred pension is. However, a married man whose wife is receiving a pension based on his contribution record cannot cancel his retirement unless she agrees, by signing the form (BR432) on which he notifies the cancellation of his retirement. Her pension, when resumed, will also be increased in line with his. DHSS leaflet NI 92 deals with the cancellation of retirement.

You can only cancel your retirement once. Once you have re-retired, you cannot cancel again.

earning while retired

Once you are getting a state pension, you will be subject to the 'earnings rule': if your earnings (after deductions for reasonable work expenses) come to more than a set maximum a week, the basic state pension you are getting will be reduced. For 1987/88, the earnings limit is £75 a week and the reduction is 5p for every 10p of earnings between £75 and £79, 5p for every 5p above that. Once a man reaches the age of 70 and a woman the age of 65, no deduction is made to their state pension, regardless of how much they earn.

An earnings-related additional pension or graduated pension increment is never reduced by the earnings rule and nor are amounts which have increased the basic pension because of deferred retirement.

A married woman whose pension is based on her husband's contribution record will lose some or all of her basic pension if she earns more than £31.45 (in 1987/88) a week. A reduction also applies where a wife has not herself retired but for whom her husband is getting a dependant's allowance: this will be reduced according to her earnings.

It is up to you to tell the local social security office whenever your earnings in any week (from sunday to saturday) exceed the current level. Leaflet NP 32 sets out what counts as earnings and what does not have to be included.

dependants

A man who has dependants when he reaches retirement age, such as a child and/or a non-earning wife under the age of 60, can claim an increase to his basic pension for the dependant(s). If his pension is a reduced one, so will be the allowance for a dependant adult. The allowance for a wife will be reduced, or wiped out, if she earns more than the weekly maximum laid down (currently £31.45). If she is not living with her husband, the allowance will only be paid if she is earning no more than the amount of the allowance, and her husband is paying her maintenance of at least that amount.

A woman can get a dependant's allowance added to her pension for her husband but only if she was getting an increase in her unemployment, sickness or invalidity benefit because of him up to the date of her retirement, if he is not getting a state benefit on his own account and is not earning more than the amount of the increase she would get for him as a dependant.

A parent who reaches retirement age while still drawing child benefit can get an increase in his or her basic pension for the child. This allowance will always be at the standard rate, even if the parent's pension is lower than the full rate.

DHSS leaflet NI 196 gives the current rates for increases, updated each year.

getting the pension

About four months before you reach pensionable age, the DHSS normally sends you a claim form, to be completed and returned to the local social security office. (If you have not received this form by three months before your birthday, ask your local social security office about it.)

In due course, you will then be sent a notice setting out what pension you are entitled to and how this is made up. If you are due to get a guaranteed minimum pension from an employer's contracted-out pension scheme, the notice will tell you the name and address of the person responsible for paying this to you. You will also be told what you need to do if you disagree with the decision about your pension payment and want to challenge the calculation.

A wife who is claiming a pension on the basis of her husband's contribution record must give notice of her 'retirement' date and complete the pension claim form within 3 months.

If you are claiming an increase in your pension because of a dependant, you have to make a separate claim for this. It is best to do this at the same time as your own claim, and in any case within 3 months of the date you become eligible for the pension, otherwise you may lose some or all of the increase.

If you are deferring your retirement, you should indicate this on the form and return it. You will be told then what pension is due to you. When you decide to retire, you should notify your local social security office approximately 4 months ahead of the time that you want to start claiming your state pension, or as soon as possible – it is not usually possible for a pension to be backdated further than 3 months.

how it is paid

The pension is payable on a weekly basis, in advance, by orders cashable at a post office. You have to specify which post office; the pension cannot be drawn from any other than the specified branch. Pensions are now payable on mondays. You do not have to collect the pension every monday: the orders can be cashed for up to three months from the date shown on each.

Alternatively, you can elect to have the pension paid directly into your bank account or National Girobank or National Savings Bank investment account or into a building society account. When the pension is to be paid in this way (called 'credit transfer'), it will be paid either 4-weekly or quarterly, in arrear. If you want to receive your pension by credit transfer, ask for form NI 105 at a social security office and complete the application form in it.

It is also possible to be sent a girocheque every quarter that you can pay yourself into any account you hold.

You will not get any pension until the first monday after your date of retirement. The first pension payments you get may turn out to be less than the full amount due to you, while the exact amount is being calculated. Any arrears will be paid to you as soon as these calculations are completed.

when you are abroad

You can generally get your retirement pension anywhere abroad. If you are going abroad for less than 3 months, you can normally let your pension build up and cash the orders when you return. But remember that a pension order can only be cashed in the 3 months after the date shown on it.

If you are going abroad for over 3 months, tell your social security office in plenty of time before you go so that they can make arrangements to get your pension paid to you abroad.

tax and the pension

Your state retirement pension, plus any additions to it (other than for a dependant child), will count as income that will have to be declared and assessed for tax.

If your income including the state pension brings you into the tax bracket, you will have to pay to the Inland Revenue each year a lump sum for the tax due on your total taxable income. If, however, you are also receiving an occupational pension or earnings from part-time employment which comes to you on the PAYE system, the tax due on your state pension will be deducted through that.

If the state basic pension were your only income, there would be no tax to pay because it is always less than the personal tax allowance.

A wife who is getting a state pension based on her own national insurance record can set her personal tax allowance (wife's earned income relief) against this, because the pension counts as her own earnings. The pension for a wife based on her husband's contribution record is treated for tax purposes as his earnings, and he has to pay the tax on it.

age allowance

Men and women when they become 64 qualify for a higher age allowance in place of the usual personal tax allowance for the tax year following the 64th birthday and thereafter. A man qualifies for this when his wife reaches the age of 64 even if he himself is younger. (But a woman does not qualify until she is 64, even though she can draw a pension at 60.)

The amounts change each year with the Budget. For the 1986/87 tax year, the age allowance was £2,850 for a single person, £4,505 for married couples.

But for every 3p by which your 'total income' exceeds a set amount (£9,400 in 1986/87), you lose 2p of the age allowance. So when income reached £10,173 for a single person, £10,675 for a married couple, the age allowance was extinguished. When that happens, the normal personal tax allowances apply instead. (In 1986/87 this was £2,335 for a single person, £3,655 for a married couple.)

'Total income' for the calculation of age allowance is normally gross income less interest payments you make which qualify for tax relief (such as a mortgage, or loan for home improvements), any payments you may be making to a personal pension, the gross amount of any covenanted payments and any enforceable maintenance payments you may be making.

Inland Revenue leaflet IR 4, available free at tax offices, explains about income tax and pensioners.

a pension from your job

The Inland revenue limits the amount of pension and other benefits that an employer's approved pension scheme (one which qualifies for tax reliefs under the Finance Act 1970) can pay. The rules are complicated; the main restrictions affecting the retirement pension you can get are

○ the maximum pension you can get at normal retirement age is two-thirds of your final remuneration, provided you have been at least 10 years with your employer

○ part of what you get may be taken as a tax-free lump sum; this must not exceed $1\frac{1}{2}$ times your final remuneration after 20 years with your employer (if fewer years, the maximum tax-free sum is smaller)

○ a pension which is being paid out can be increased beyond the initial limit up to the amount needed to keep it in line with inflation (related to the retail price index)

○ the maximum total contribution you may pay into an employer's scheme in any year is 15% of your remuneration in that year.

Schemes tend not to be as generous as the Inland Revenue would allow: it would be extraordinary to be able to clock up in total more than the maximum allowed.

the pension you may get

Until the Social Security Act 1986 comes fully into force in April 1988, bringing in the possibility of more alternatives to non-state pensions, anyone in employment who has been participating in an employer's pension scheme, whether contributory or non-contributory will, on retirement, get a pension based either on 'final pay' or on a 'money purchase' basis. Some employers provide a choice between the two, according to which will at the time of retirement provide the higher amount. A very few schemes are based on average pay or on salary grades during the years in the scheme, or provide a fixed sum for each year of membership.

Whichever type of scheme, ask the firm's pensions manager a few months in advance of your retirement date what yours will produce for you.

final pay scheme

In a final pay scheme, the pension is worked out according to a formula and depends on your earnings near retirement and the number of years you have belonged to the scheme. If you stay in one scheme until retirement, your eventual pension should have kept pace with increases in your earnings.

On retirement your pension will be worked out on

○ the number of years that count as pensionable
   (usually the length of time you have been a member of the scheme; some schemes relate pension to total service with the employer, which may be longer than the period of actual membership of the scheme)
○ your earnings at or around the time you retire
○ the proportion of earnings for each year in the scheme
   (for example, you may get a pension of 1/60th of your earnings for each year of membership or 1/80th for each year, depending on the particular scheme).

The 'final pay' on which your pension will be based is usually not your exact salary at the time you retire, but your pensionable earnings over some specified years. (The definition of 'pensionable earnings' varies from scheme to scheme; it is the figure used as the basis for contributions payable and for calculating the pension.)

The definition of 'final pay' is normally expressed in terms of salary over a period ending at the date of retirement. This avoids situations where a member has his salary rate increased just before retirement as a device to enhance his pension benefits.

'Final pay' may, for example, be defined as

○ basic pay at the date on which yearly pay rises are usually made in that firm

○ the yearly average of total earnings during a specified number of recent years
○ highest basic pay during the last so-many years, plus the average of extras such as bonuses, commission and overtime during a specified period
○ the yearly average of the best 3 consecutive years' earnings out of the last so-many years.

Where the scheme's definition is annual average earnings of last 3 years, for example, it means that for someone retiring on a final salary of £10,000 a year, having earned £10,000 for 6 months, £9,500 for 12 months, £9,000 for 12 months and £8,500 for 6 months, the scheme's final pensionable salary comes to £9,250 – which is $7\frac{1}{2}$% less than salary at date of retirement. This can cause disappointment when someone expects to get a pension based on the salary he is receiving at the time he retires.

If your employer's scheme is contracted out of the state earnings-related pension scheme, you will get only the basic state pension on top of your employer's pension. Your employer's pension, however, must provide you with at least as much (and generally much more, under the legislation governing contracted-out schemes before November 1986) as the state's earnings-related pension would be for you.

money purchase scheme
In a money purchase scheme, the pension you get depends on the amount of money paid in by you, and by your employers for you, and how this has built up through the scheme's investments by the time you retire. This fund is used then to provide you with a pension, usually through an annuity bought for you from an insurance company. An annuity is an arrangement whereby a lump sum is paid to a life insurance company in return for a regular income to be paid for the rest of the annuitant's life.

Your pension at retirement will depend on how the contributions have grown through investment and on interest rates and their effect on annuity rates at the time you retire.

How large an annuity can be bought with your lump sum is worked out on an actuarial basis – that is, an assumption of how long a person of your age and sex and health is likely to live. For the same payment, a woman may receive up to one-third less than a man because of the use of different mortality tables for men and women.

The annuity will also depend on interest rates generally at the time it is taken out. Because of variations in interest rates, different people can get dramatically different pensions for the same level of contributions.

You have to rely on the trustees of the scheme to select the insurance company that at the time will bring you the best annuity. Your annuity will not be affected by changes in rates after it is bought: the same size payments will continue throughout the rest of its (i.e. your) life. It depends on the scheme's rules whether you have the right to any say in the annuity to be bought.

In some money purchase schemes, the pension fund itself provides the pension. An annuity is not bought from an insurance company but the scheme's trustees assume an annuity rate (generally in line with insurance companies' rates) to use as the basis of how much pension to pay you. The payments are made straight out of the fund, the remaining money remains invested and continues to accrue a return.

effect of the state pension

Many occupational pension schemes take account of the pension you will be getting from the state when calculating the pension they will pay you. For example, the amount of the single person's basic state pension may be deducted as part of the calculations of what are your pensionable earnings. (In such a case, your contributions to the employer's scheme are likely to have been based on earnings which ignored a first 'slice' of your earnings roughly equal to the amount of the single person's current state pension. This is referred to as 'integration', with the state scheme.)

You should find out (if you do not already know) whether this is what your employer's scheme does, so that you can check the calculation of your own pension accurately. Integration can make quite a difference to the amount you get: an integrated scheme paying 1/60th of final pensionable earnings may produce less than a scheme paying 1/80th without deduction for the state pension.

At present, a money purchase scheme cannot be contracted-out of the state earnings-related pension scheme (because it cannot guarantee to produce a given pension at retirement). So, employees who have been members of a money purchase scheme get a two-tier pension from the state: the basic pension plus the earnings-related addition.

lump sum on retirement

With most employer's schemes, you have the option of commuting part of the pension that is due to you into a lump sum payment. With some schemes, mostly in the public sector, a lump sum is paid automatically on retirement as well as a pension.

With most schemes, the pension is reduced if you opt to take the lump sum. The amount of pension you will have to forgo depends on the rules of the particular scheme. It may be a fixed ratio – usually, 9 : 1 for a man and 11 : 1 for a woman. A man would thereby lose £100 a year of his due pension for each £900 of lump sum taken at the time of his retirement; a woman would be allowed to take £1,100 of lump sum for the loss of £100 from her annual pension (on the assumption that she will live longer and would therefore have to be paid a pension for longer).

With some schemes, a standard cash-to-pension ratio is not used and the actual amount that has to be forgone for the amount taken as a lump sum depends on interest rates at time you retire. So you cannot calculate accurately in advance how much pension you will lose in order to get the lump sum you would like to have on retirement.

You do not have to pay tax on any lump sum that is part of a pension package but the Inland Revenue restrict the sum that a pension scheme can let anyone take. The maximum depends on how many years you have worked for the employer on the basis of 1/80ths of your final remuneration for each year.

number of years in scheme	maximum lump sum as 80ths of final pay
1	3
2	6
3	9
4	12
5	15
6	18
7	21
8	24
9	30
10	36
11	42
12	48
13	54
14	63
15	72
16	81
17	90
18	99
19	108
20 or more	120

So, the highest lump sum you could take would be 120/80ths of, or $1\frac{1}{2}$ times, your final remuneration.

These are the maximum amounts allowed by the Inland Revenue and do not necessarily correspond with a scheme's rules (which may allow only a smaller lump sum).

example

Joseph retires at the age of 65. His final remuneration comes to £18,000. He has belonged to the pension scheme for 17 years. His pension is based on the 1/60th formula, so will be £5,100 a year. But he can swap part of it for a lump sum. The maximum sum he can take tax-free under the Inland Revenue rules is 90/80ths of the amount of his final remuneration; the rules of his firms's pension scheme also permit this. So, the biggest lump sum he can take is

$$90/80 \times £18,000 = £20,250.$$

He loses £100 of pension for each £900 of lump sum. If he takes the maximum lump sum, his pension will come down to

$$£5,100 - £2,250 (£20,250 \div 9) = £2,850 \text{ a year.}$$

If you belong to a scheme which is contracted-out of the state additional pension scheme, you will not be able to take a lump sum which is so large that it would reduce your pension to below the guaranteed minimum pension level.

A lump sum can be taken only at the time of retirement; once the pension has started to be paid, it cannot be commuted.

Taking the lump sum is nearly always advantageous: you can invest it or use it to buy an annuity and so increase your income in retirement.

Any future increases in the pension you draw from the scheme will be related to the pension you are actually receiving, not to the pension you would have had if you had not given up part of it for cash. If you, therefore, do not wish to take the maximum permitted lump sum, you can take just a part of it.

If the pension you will be getting is inflation-proofed, so that it will be increased regularly in line with the retail price index, this is such a valuable asset that you should be wary of exchanging any part of your pension for a lump sum when you retire. But if future increases in your pension are likely to be infrequent and unpredictable, it could be better to exchange as much as possible for a lump sum and invest it. If you use at least part of the sum to buy yourself an annuity, this will produce a regular income for the rest of your life. Moreover, the whole of the pension from your employer's scheme will be taxable, and only part of the income from an annuity you have bought yourself from an insurance company will be taxable, so you may get a higher net income from your annuity than from the pension.

future increases in the pension

What increases will be made to the pension you will be getting in the years after retirement depends on the rules of the particular scheme. If you work in the public sector (for central or local government, in a nationalised industry, or as a teacher or police-man, for example), your whole pension is likely to go up annually by the percentage of price inflation during the preceding 12 months. Very few pension schemes outside the public sector are fully inflation-proofed.

Some schemes will increase pensions by, say, 3% or 5% com-pound a year. A few schemes undertake to increase pensions partially in line with inflation each year – by, say, two-thirds of the rise in the retail price index (RPI, the official measure of the general level of prices).

It is more common for schemes not to guarantee a set increase but to review the position from time to time and to make dis-cretionary increases of varying amounts. With some schemes, increases are generous in the sense of getting close to complete inflation-proofing. You may get a mixture: low fixed increases plus discretionary ones.

Increases do not depend on the pensioners' circumstances but on the financial health of the fund and other demands on it. Where such increases are not financed from the existing fund, they depend on what the employer can afford at the time. Many schemes do not fund in advance for discretionary increases, but rely on extra contributions from the employer at the time each increase is made.

If the scheme is a money purchase one, it may be possible to arrange to buy an increasing annuity in which the amount you get paid will increase regularly. Or part of the fund might be held back to pay for increases when the pension is being paid to you.

If the scheme you belong to is a contracted-out one, the state will pay you any additional amounts required to increase the 'guaranteed minimum pension' part of your pension each year after retirement to keep it in line with price inflation. These increases will be paid along with your state pension.

making additional contributions

Many occupational pension schemes have allowed members to make additional contributions to the scheme on a voluntary basis. From April 1988 legislation will require all employer's to provide this facility.

You can start making voluntary contributions at any time. These must not bring your total contributions to the scheme to more than 15% of your taxable pay each year, but since your regular contributions are unlikely to be more than 3% or 4% of your pay, you can be paying as much as 10% to 12% in voluntary contributions, if you want to.

Additional voluntary contributions (AVCs) have the great advantage that they are paid out of pre-tax income, in the same way as your regular contributions. Also, the investment returns are not subject to tax. So they can be a tax-efficient way of enhancing your pension particularly if you are approaching retirement and have not been a member of your employer's pension scheme for long enough to qualify for the full benefits.

AVC schemes are usually on a money purchase basis: your contributions are invested and build up to provide a tax-free sum of money. When you come to retire, this can then be used to 'buy' any extra benefits you want within the scheme's rules and subject to the Inland Revenue limits. For example, AVCs may 'buy' extra years of membership in the scheme to increase the pension you become eligible for, or provide a fixed addition to the pension, or be taken as a tax-free lump sum, or to guarantee increases in the pension after retirement. Some schemes are more flexible than others about the benefits you can have from AVCs, so find out exactly what you can get from yours.

If you want a lump sum, it may be better to take the sum accumulated from your AVCs as a lump sum and keep the pension you are due intact, rather than commuting part of it to get a lump sum. In this way, you will not lose out on any annual increases to the pension.

early retirement

An important point is to know when you can retire and take your pension from the firm's scheme. This is not necessarily the same time as the state pension will become due. Most occupational pension schemes, however, do fix their 'normal retirement age' at 65 for men and 60 for women.

If you retire before the scheme's normal retirement age, your pension will be smaller. The reason is that the pension will probably have to be paid to you for more years than if you retired at normal retirement age, and the fund (contributions and interest) will have had less time to build up.

A pension might, for example, be the amount built up so far, minus $\frac{1}{2}$% for each month of early retirement. Or it may be reduced according to a scale, say

> minus 2% for retiring 3 years early
> 5% for retiring 4 years early
> 9% for retiring 5 years early.

Some schemes reduce the pension depending on the person's age, length of service and individual circumstances.

In general, the Inland Revenue allows a scheme to pay out on voluntary early retirement only if you have reached the age of 50.

But a woman can take early retirement from the age of 45 if the scheme's normal retirement age is less than 60 and she is within ten years of it.

If you are thinking of retiring early, make sure that you are fully aware of the way your employer's pension scheme deals with this situation. Ask for details of the basis on which your early pension will be calculated so that you know the facts and figures before you make your decision and at a time when you can still do something about the pension.

Even retiring just five years early could reduce your occupational pension by one-third.

postponed retirement

If your employer agrees, you may be able to go on working and put off your retirement beyond the normal age. Usually, your pension is then worked out as if you had retired at the normal time, but will be increased when you do retire to take account of the period for which you postponed retiring.

The enhanced pension cannot normally exceed the usual Inland Revenue limit of two-thirds of final remuneration at the normal retirement date. But if you clock up more than 40 years' service with your employer, the pension can be increased for each year in excess of 40 which you work after normal retirement date. The Inland Revenue rules allow an extra one-sixtieth per year to accrue for those extra years, up to a maximum allowable pension of 45/60ths – that is, three-quarters of final remuneration at the date of normal retirement.

Within this limit, the amount by which the pension will be increased by postponing retirement depends on the formula used by the particular scheme. The formula takes account of the long-term investment returns and the fact that the pension will have to be paid for less time. A factor of 9% is common for the rate of increase for each year of deferment.

Normally, contributions stop at normal retirement age. The scheme may allow you to make contributions beyond this age and so earn further one-eightieths or one-sixtieths. In a money purchase scheme, it is unlikely that the employer will make further contributions.

pension from previous employers' scheme

If you had contributed to the scheme of employers for whom you no longer work and when you left their employ you had 'preverved' your pension in their scheme, you should write to the trustees of that scheme, or the firm's pensions manager or administrator, about four months before you are due to retire, saying that you will be retiring on such-and-such a date and will be claiming your pension from the scheme then. Ask what the pension will be, how it will be paid, what options there are (for example, commutation to a lump sum), and the tax position.

A preserved pension is usually payable from the normal pension age of the scheme in which it was earned, so you can claim this pension even if you have not yet reached the retirement age of your present employer's scheme. If you retire from your final job earlier than the retirement date of the preserved pension scheme, you may be able to arrange that the preserved pension can start to be paid then (but this may be at a lower rate). If you work beyond the normal retirement date of the first scheme, the rules of that scheme will say whether payment can start nevertheless or whether it must be deferred to your actual retirement.

just before you retire

How a pension scheme works is laid down in its trust deeds and rules. These are complicated documents, written in legal language (difficult to understand and interpret without expert help). Any member of the scheme has the right to be provided with certain information about the scheme, including how contribution levels are calculated, and the benefits. (Additional information must be made available on request.) On retirement, a member must be told the amount of benefit to which he or she is entitled, the conditions relating to payment and any provision for benefit increases.

You should ahve been given an explanatory booklet about the scheme when you first joined it, and been sent a note of any changes in the rules since then. Get out this document and any interim ones you may have had, and go through them carefully to make sure that you understand on what basis your pension entitlement will be worked out, and what other benefits may be available.

About three months before you are due to retire, you will need details about what your pension will be exactly, about the effect of swapping part of it for a lump sum (if the scheme offers this option) and about how it will be paid and taxed. Full information and a detailed statement should be given to you as a matter of course.

You should also check that the person you nominated as beneficiary or dependant for any sum payable from the scheme on your death is still the one you want to receive this. The rules of the scheme are likely to define who will get any dependant's pension but the trustees usually have discretion about the payment of any lump sum, and your wishes should be made clear about this.

When you have gone through all the information available about your pension and other payments, you should [try to] arrange a meeting with the pensions manager or administrator.

There are bound to be some points about which you are not clear and there may be options on which you have to make a positive decision. It will be useful to prepare in advance a list of all the points you need to know and want to discuss. These may include

o how much your pension will come to (gross or net)
o the basis for the calculation
o how it will be paid and when
o if you have been making additional voluntary contributions, how much has accrued and what this sum can be used for
o if it is a money purchase scheme, what is the amount available to buy an annuity? what are current annuity rates? where is it proposed to buy the annuity for you?
o if you can exchange part of your pension for a lump sum now, how large can this be (including from any AVCs)? by how much will this (or any lesser amount you choose to take) reduce your pension?
o if a widow/er's pension is provided, how much will it be? can you arrange for it to be more? if so, how much of your own pension will you have to give up for this?
o if a widow/er's pension is not automatically provided by the scheme, can you arrange that a pension will be paid to him or her? if so, how much could this be and how much of your own pension would you have to give up for this?
o can any dependant other than a spouse get a pension on your death? if so, how much might this be and to whom could it be paid?
o what increases are likely to be made to your pension once you have retired?

If you are married, it would be sensible to share all the information about your pension arrangements with your wife or husband, particularly the name and address of the person to notify if you should die first, and what pension should thereafter be provided for your widow(er).

calculating how much you will get

If it is a final pay scheme, you should be told what the scheme's definition of pensionable earnings produces for you. This will be the figure produced by the calculation of 1/60th (or 1/80th) × years in the scheme × final pensionable earnings. Remember that final pensionable earnings is not the same as the salary you are receiving at the moment of retirement but is based on the scheme's definition of 'final remuneration'.

money purchase scheme

With a money purchase scheme, you will not necessarily be told precisely how much is available for buying your annuity, but you should be given at least an approximation of both that and how much pension it will produce for you, and told which insurance company, or other source, it will come from. A few pension schemes use their own funds to provide money purchase pensions.

How much the money that has accumulated for you can buy by way of annuity depends on the annuity rate at the time it is bought. You can ask to see competitive quotations from insurance companies – they all have different rates. A poor rate at the time will mean a (comparatively) less good pension for the rest of your life. It is unlikely that the scheme rules would allow you to postpone taking a money purchase pension if interest rates are low at the time of your retirement. What you might do is to take as large a lump sum as Inland Revenue rules allow, invest it temporarily and convert it to an annuity later.

a lump sum

Where taking a lump sum is optional, you should be told by how much your pension will be reduced per £100 of lump sum you take. Under Inland Revenue rules, the maximum a scheme can let you take is $1\frac{1}{2}$ times your final remuneration.

Before coming to a decision whether to take a lump sum, you should bear in mind the effect of future inflation and that you could be retired for as long as 20 years or more. You should consider whether the lower pension resulting from turning some of it into a cash payment on retirement will leave you and your family enough to live on, not just in the early years of your retirement but later on. You should take into account your likely income from any other sources (state pension, investments, part-time job) and your age and health. An income which seems adequate now could be severely eroded by the effect of inflation over the years.

If you take a lump sum, you may be able to invest it to produce a better overall income than the pension you would get from the employer's scheme if you left it intact. But where a scheme's pension is fully inflation-proofed, you are unlikely to be able to invest the sum in such a way as to provide a better income. For example, if you exchange £1 of inflation-proof pension for £9 of lump sum, you would need a return on your investment of around 11% above inflation and before tax, in order not to lose out. If your employer's scheme usually increases pensions in payment by around 3% a year, you would need to be able to invest the lump sum at a return of about 14% before tax in order not to lose out.

The main advantage of taking a cash sum out of your pension lies in the tax benefit: the lump sum will be tax free, your pension will be taxed as earned income.

If you do not expect your pension to be increased much over the years, you could do better by taking the tax-free cash and using it to buy an annuity for yourself. The income from an annuity bought by an individual (rather than by a pension scheme on behalf of one of its members) is treated as partly return of capital and partly interest, and only the interest element is taxable. So, taking a cash sum and buying an annuity would mean that you pay less tax than on the untouched pension.

Once an annuity has been bought, however, the money has gone beyond recall: you cannot later forgo the income to get back any remaining capital.

tax on your pension

Your pension from all sources will count as earned income and will be taxed at your normal rate.

The pension from your employer's scheme will be paid to you with tax deducted, as your salary has been, through the PAYE system. But you will notice that a larger amount of tax than you would have expected is taken from the pension payment. This is because the tax due on your state pension (which will be paid to you in full without any deduction for tax) will also be taken from your occupational pension.

If you buy an annuity yourself, the insurance company will notify you how much of the payment is capital (tax-free) and how much is interest (taxable), so that you can enter this on your tax return. The insurance company will deduct tax at the basic rate from the interest part of the payment to you. If you are a higher rate taxpayer, you will get a tax demand for the further tax due; if you are a non-taxpayer, you will have to reclaim the deducted tax from the Inland Revenue (or may be able to arrange for the annuity payment to be made gross).

personal tax allowances

Men and women over the age of 64 get a higher personal allowance against income tax than younger people. This is called 'age allowance' and applies from the start of the tax year in which you have your 65th birthday. A married couple get age allowance if one or both were over 64 at the start of the tax year.

You will lose £2 of age allowance for every £3 by which your total income exceeds a certain limit set for each tax year. The allowance will not be reduced below the normal personal tax allowance (single or married).

sources of information

There are several organisations which can provide information on various aspects of occupational pensions. These include the

○ Company Pensions Information Centre
  7 Old Park Lane, London W1Y 3LJ (telephone: 01-493 4757)
  The CPIC publishes a number of leaflets (free, but send a large self-addressed stamped envelope) for members of pension schemes. It can provide information generally about occupational pensions but cannot be asked to intervene in disputes between an individual and a particular pension scheme.

○ Occupational Pensions Advisory Service
  room 327, Aviation House, 129 Kingsway, London WC2B 6NN (telephone: 01-405 6922 ext 205)
  OPAS is an independent body, registered as a charity, set up with the objective of proffering advice and assistance on all matters relating to occupational pension schemes to individuals, and particularly beneficiaries with specific problems regarding the scheme they belong to. OPAS is not an arbitration service but can try to clarify the information provided by a scheme to anyone who does not understand or is dissatisfied, and will intervene on an individual's behalf where necessary. There are OPAS advisers in many parts of the country, as well as a central panel of pension experts. They can be contacted either direct or through a local advisory body, notably the CAB.

  OPAS advisers do not offer personal financial advice, but can explain the broad implications of a choice to be made under the rules of a particular pension scheme. There is no charge for the advice and help provided by OPAS.

○ Occupational Pensions Board
  Lynwood House, Thames Ditton, Surrey KT7 0DP (telephone: 01-398 4242)
  The OPB is a government established body, primarily to supervise occupational pension schemes, particularly those contracted out of the state earnings-related pension scheme. The

OPB publishes occasional leaflets on individual rights, but cannot take up individual queries.

○ Trades Union Congress
Congress House, Great Russell Street, London WC1B 3LS (telephone: 01-636 4030)
As well as publications such as *A guide to occupational pension schemes* (£1), the TUC can advise and help TU members with pension problems, either direct or through the trade union representative.

○ National Association of Pension Funds
12–18 Grosvenor Gardens, London SW1W 0DH (telephone: 01-730 0585)
This is an organisation primarily for trustees and administrators of pension funds, but some of its publications are useful by providing general information about the way pension funds operate.

○ Association of Pension Lawyers
Secretary: J J Quarrell, 76 Jermyn Street, London SW1Y 6NR
Members of this association are particularly concerned with the legal aspects of pension arrangements and are experienced practitioners in pension cases. A list of members is available from the Secretary.

A citizens advice bureau may be able to help with preliminary advice on a problem, and will know where you should turn for further help. Also a local branch of Age Concern can be asked for advice; addresses of branches are available from Age Concern's information department at Bernard Sunley House, 60 Pitcairn Road, Mitcham, Surrey CR4 3LI (telephone 01-640 5431).

a personally arranged pension

If you have been self-employed all your working life (paying class 2 national insurance contributions) you will not be eligible for the earnings-related addition to the basic state pension, nor will you have had access to an occupational pension scheme. To compensate for this, the Inland Revenue allow special tax concessions on a self-employed person's payments into any personal pension scheme approved by IR – officially a 'retirement annuity contract'.

You can also pay into such a scheme when you are an employee but do not contribute to an employer's pension scheme (either because there is none or you have chosen not to join a voluntary scheme) or if you have freelance earnings in addition to your salary.

Personal pension schemes are basically savings plans or policies run by insurance companies, banks, building societies and similar organisations which are 'approved' under financial services legislation. You pay premiums, either regularly or in lump sums at intervals, to the organisation which invests the money. When you retire, the company uses the invested money to provide you with a pension until you die. Part of the accumulated money can usually be exchanged for a tax-free lump sum on retirement.

Once you have invested in one of these schemes, you cannot usually get at your money until you retire and draw the pension.

types of pension plans

How the pension you get from the money invested in a pension plan will be worked out depends on the type of plan as well as on the insurance company, bank, building society or other organisation you have invested with. There are two main methods of calculating the pension.

○ *deferred annuity plan*
The amount of pension you will get will have been decided when you took out the policy: £x of pension for £y of premiums. For example, paying £1,000 a year for 10 years from the age of 55, will produce a pension of £1,500 a year when you retire at the age of 65.

○ *cash-funded plan*
The accumulated fund from your invested premiums will be used to buy an annuity at the time you retire. So, the pension you get will depend on the amount you have paid in premiums, the return on the investment of the premiums by the insurance company, annuity rates at the time you retire. For example, if you have been paying £1,000 a year in premiums from the age of 50 and, by the time you reach 65, the accumulated fund has grown to £20,000 and at that time annuity rates are 10 per cent, your pension will be £2,000 a year.

You may want to delay your retirement for a year or two if annuity rates are particularly poor, or the stock market particularly depressed, at the time you had planned to retire.

paying premiums
With nearly all pension policies, you can pay either regular annual premiums or a one-off single premium. Either method can be used, whether the pension will be on the basis of a deferred annuity or a cash-funded one.

With regular premiums, you are committed to paying a fixed amount to the insurance company each year until retirement date. The terms of a particular policy may allow you to vary the amount of each payment or even to miss one occasionally – an important advantage for someone who is self-employed whose earnings vary from year to year. Otherwise, if you find yourself unable to continue the premiums, the policy will be made 'paid up', for which the insurance company will levy a charge, and your pension at retirement will be proportionately reduced.

With a single premium policy, there is no further commitment beyond the payment of the one premium to the insurance company. You can make payments at different times to different companies. The commission payable on a single premium policy is a smaller percentage than on a regular-premium policy.

If in the years leading up to your retirement, you decide you want to increase your potential pension, you would probably get a better return by paying a single premium for a policy rather than starting out on regular premium payments.

premiums and tax

Inland Revenue rules permit only a set percentage of 'net relevant earnings' to be paid each year into a personal pension scheme. The maximum is currently $17\frac{1}{2}\%$ for anyone born in 1934 or later, 20% or more for anyone born before 1934.

'Net relevant earnings' for tax relief purposes are broadly defined by the Inland Revenue as "profits immediately derived by an individual from a trade or profession and earnings from non-pensionable employment", minus certain deductions to make them 'net'. These deductions include business losses, agreed capital allowances, and expenses which cannot be set off against any other income.

There is special tax relief on the premiums you pay to an Inland Revenue approved retirement annuity contract – that is, a personal pension plan. The premiums can be paid out of pre-tax income, which means that you get relief at your highest rate of tax.

'carry forward'

Inland Revenue rules enable you to carry forward any tax relief not made use of during the previous six years. If premiums paid in respect of any of these years did not reach your limit for that year (the set percentage of your net relevant earnings), the balance of relief can be carried forward so that in the current year, you can pay more than that year's maximum percentage of your earnings (if you can afford to). For example, within the tax year 1987/88, you would be able to mop up any tax relief you had not made use of in any of the preceding six years – 1981/82 to 1986/87 inclusive – in addition to the premium that you can pay to the maximum percentage limit for 1987/88. This means that all the premiums you pay in 1987/88 will be taken off your gross earnings, reducing your taxable income in that year.

In the years leading up to your retirement, you should check whether premiums paid in previous years were less than the maximum for the year in which they were made and calculate accordingly how much you could carry forward to increase your payment in the coming years.

Anyone who is making payments to personal pension plans should keep a record year by year of net relevant earnings. (A self-employed person can get this figure from his accountant at the end of his accounting year; an employed person can tell from his P60 from his employer at the end of the tax year.) Against this earnings figure, you should put the amount of premium(s) you have paid in the year, the percentage this is of your net relevant earnings for the year, and by how much this was less than the maximum figure allowed for tax relief for that tax year. Then you can take advantage of the carry-forward provisions in any year when you can pay more than that year's maximum for tax relief, and can tell the Inland Revenue how much is to be used from which of the past six years.

'carry back'

There are also what are called 'carry back' provisions. These allow a premium paid in any one tax year to be treated for tax purposes as if it had been paid in the previous year provided you make the requisite 'election' in time. The election has to be made within the year of assessment during which the premium is paid. The timing of the election is crucial: if a premium paid in the year 1987/88 is to be treated for tax purposes as being paid in the tax year 1986/87, the election for this would have to be made before 5 April 1988, by notifying your local tax inspector (in writing or by using form 43 available at tax offices).

If you want and can afford to pay as much as possible in any one year, you can combine the advantages of carrying-forward and carrying-back. If you had not paid as much in the way of premium as you could have in the previous year, you can pay more than your maximum in the current year and elect to carry back the appropriate part of that payment to be allocated to the previous tax year. If you had no net relevant earnings at all in any previous tax year, you can skip that year and elect to carry back to the year before that.

the policies you may have

There are three main types of pension policy which you may have been paying into or now want to start paying into.

with-profits policy
The insurance company or bank, or building society etc, will have guaranteed from the outset the minimum pension it will pay you or the minimum amount of money that will be available to you for buying an annuity at the time you have decided you want to retire (which has to be specified when you first take out the policy). But according to the profits it makes on its investment, the company announces increases from time to time in the guaranteed amount. These increases are called 'reversionary bonuses'. Once a bonus has been declared, it cannot be taken away.

In addition, most insurance companies add to their with-profits policies a 'terminal bonus' (or it may be called 'maturity bonus', 'final bonus', 'vesting bonus', 'capital bonus') at the time the policy is encashed. This terminal bonus is never guaranteed and you will not know how much it may be, or whether one will be paid, until the moment comes. Sometimes, the final bonus ends up providing a higher proportion of the total payment at retirement than the guaranteed minimum amount plus the reversionary bonuses that have been added throughout the life of the policy.

unit-linked policy
With a 'unit-linked' policy, every premium paid buys units in a selected fund or funds. The funds are managed by the insurance company and are invested in different sectors of the investment

market. Some funds are very specialised, some cover a broad range of sectors, spreading the risk for the investor.

There are, for instance:

○ property funds
○ equity funds (stocks and shares, often in a specific market)
○ fixed-interest funds (e.g. british government stock, company loan stock)
○ cash funds (e.g. bank deposit accounts, local authority short-term loans).
○ managed, or mixed, funds, where the money is invested in a spread of sectors.

A few unit-linked policies guarantee a minimum sum when you cash the policy (for example, not less than the total premiums paid) and some guarantee a minimum annuity rate on retirement. But such guarantees tend to be low, often related to building societies' mortgage rates.

Nearly all unit-linked policies are on a cash-funded basis, so the amount of pension you get will depend not only on how well the investments have done but on annuity rates at the time you want to draw on the fund for a pension.

One of the problems with a unit-linked pension policy is that the retirement time is fixed (at the age of 60 or 65, say) and at that time investment conditions may make it a bad time to cash in the units. You may feel it prudent, therefore, when retirement is, say, two or three years away, to switch your units into a guaranteed fund, and to invest the last two or three years' premiums likewise. This will produce a guaranteed return and the fund is certain to grow over the last two or three crucial years before you come to draw a pension. It is important to check in good time whether your policy has such a switching facility – and then remember to exercise the switch option as retirement approaches and to time it well (that is, when unit prices are high). A number of insurance companies do draw attention to their guaranteed fund when sending out renewal literature to those policyholders who are nearing retirement.

deposit administration scheme

These 'policies' operate in a similar manner to an investment account at a bank or building society. Your premiums go into an account with the insurance company, to which interest is added at regular intervals. The interest rate will vary according to the general level of interest rates. Different insurance companies use different methods of allocating and calculating the interest that is applied to each policyholder's deposit administration account. Customarily, the interest rate is linked to a quoted index: this may be building societies' current mortgage rates or the return on fixed interest investments. A few companies lay down a minimum interest rate.

The insurance company will deduct its charges from the premiums received; some have an annual management charge, others make a straight deduction (of up to 5%) from the initial premium. With most companies, differing percentages of premium are allocated to the fund according to the age of the policyholder and the length of time to retirement. All deposit administration schemes are cash-funded; a few of them guarantee that the cash produced by the scheme at the time you retire will be not less than a specified amount.

tax

With all types of approved pension policies, no tax is charged on the fund accumulating through the investment of the premiums paid. And any cash sum you take in lieu of some of the pension when you come to retire is tax-free. So, taking into account also the tax relief on the premiums you are paying, these pension schemes are a very efficient way of saving for your retirement.

when you come to retire

Under Inland Revenue rules, the pension from an approved policy must start being paid out before the policyholder reaches the age of 75, and (except for people in specific occupation categories) cannot start to be paid out before the age of 60. Within this age band, you can choose at what age you want the policy to pay out.

Flexibility in choosing the time when you start drawing a pension is an advantage that a personal pension policy has over an employed person's occupational pension scheme. If you have a number of policies, for differing periods of time, you can draw on each in turn, to increase your income over the first decade or so of retirement. Some pension plans can be taken out as a series of separate policies, each one maturing at a different date so that you can phase your 'retirement' by taking an increasing amount of pension over so-many years. With some policies, you have to say at the outset when you intend to retire. Others have a standard retirement age but may allow you to retire when you like within a given age range.

Many personal pension contracts are drawn up with the age of 70 as the starting date for payment. If you want to draw on it earlier, the insurance company may levy a charge because investments are being realised earlier than expected. It would be wise to have at least one contract with a retirement age of, say, 60 in case you do want to start getting a pension early or choose one that does not impose a penalty charge for earlier encashment. The same outlay will buy a larger pension, the later the retirement age specified in the contract.

There is no need literally to 'retire'. The contracts are insurance policies and there are no conditions on what your circumstances are when you draw on one, provided you are within the time limits specified. As a self-employed person, you may want to continue to work when you are over sixty, but in a reduced capacity, augmenting your lower earnings by a pension payment.

retiring younger

In certain occupations, self-employed people are not normally expected by the Inland Revenue rules to work until the age of 60, because of the physical requirements of the job or because of the continual stress under which the work is done. There is a published list of occupations for which the Inland Revenue have agreed an early retirement age.

If you should want to draw a pension before the normal age specified in your policy, because ill health prevents you from going on working at your normal occupation, you would need to provide the insurance company with evidence of your genuine incapacity (usually a doctor's report will be required) so that they can comply with Inland Revenue rules for paying out a pension early. The pension you get will be a reduced one, based on actuarial calculations: if the reduction seems to you disproportionate, you should try challenging the calculation.

In no other circumstances can you draw on a retirement annuity contract before the age specified in the policy.

retiring later

You may have been pessimistic, or over protective of your future self, when you took out a policy and chose a retirement age which, now you are reaching it, seems too soon and you are able to go on earning sufficiently not to need the pension when you thought you might. You can postpone the moment for drawing on the policy for as long as you like up to your 75th birthday; the amount of your eventual pension will increase accordingly for every year of delayed retirement or, with a cash-funded policy, the fund available to buy you an annuity will be greater – and the rate you get will be better, the older you are.

option to transfer

A cash-funded policy taken out since 1978 will almost certainly include what is called an 'open market' option (and many of those taken out earlier have been amended to include a slightly restricted version of the option). This enables a policyholder who has built up a cash fund with one insurance company to use it on retirement to buy an annuity from an insurance company that is at that time offering a better rate of return on annuities. Having been told what cash sum is available, you can undertake a 'shopping' exercise to find out where this will buy you the best pension: the insurance company which has produced a good return on investments may not be offering the best rates for a retirement annuity at the date of your retirement.

The option also provides the opportunity to consolidate the funds built up from various single-premium policies.

Some insurance companies encourage policyholders to stay with them by offering a bonus of between 1% and 5% on the accrued fund if it is not taken away but is used to buy an annuity from that company; some penalise policyholders who do take up the option, by making a charge of 5% of the value of the fund for arranging to do so.

Taking any bonus or penalty into account, you should check the annuity market at the time to find out whether better terms are available from another company.

What you should ask for is a quotation for a 'substituted contract'. The rates for these differ slightly from those for other immediate annuities so it is important that you specify that what you want is a quotation for a substituted contract. The insurance company then knows that the funds for the annuity are coming from an approved pension policy and that the annuity will therefore be liable for tax on the total payment, as would an annuity from the original insurance company.

The rates for substituted annuities are quoted regularly in the financial magazines (*Planned Savings, Money Management*, for example) or you could telephone a selection of life insurance companies yourself and ask for a quotation. You may, however, prefer to consult a specialist life or pensions broker, who should get you a range of comparable quotations.

In theory, the decision whether or not to take up the option should be a simple calculation:

1 ask the insurance company you have been paying premiums to how much has accumulated in your fund
2 ask what pension this would produce if left with that company
3 check if there would be a charge if you transferred your fund (or a bonus if you do not)
4 obtain quotations for a substituted annuity contract from a number of other insurance companies
5 if (4) produces a figure greater than (2), adjusted by (3), the option to transfer should be taken.

If you choose to transfer your fund to a different company, the money will not be paid to you (the law does not permit this) but will be passed by the original insurance company direct to the insurance company you have selected to provide the annuity (and a lump sum, if you want to commute some of the fund to this), which then deals with you according to the terms of the substituted contract.

taking a lump sum

When you come to the point of wanting to draw on a personal pension policy, you will be faced with the decision of how much (if any) of the amount available under the policy you would like to commute into a cash payment there and then instead of using it all to provide you with a pension through the insurance company (or a substituted company).

The Inland Revenue permits only part of the money available to be taken as a lump sum, which is tax-free. The maximum is three times the pension that will be produced by the sum remaining after commutation. For example, if the policy would produce a pension of £7,000 a year, you could instead take a lump sum of £15,000 and have an annual pension of £5,000.

Although you may think it wise to have the highest possible assured income for your retirement, it can be advantageous to take a cash sum in lieu of part of your potential pension. This is because the whole of the pension that emanates from a personal pension policy is taxed as earned income. But if you yourself use your own cash to buy what is called a 'purchased life annuity', not all the income that results from this is taxable: the capital element is tax-free so you are liable for tax only on the interest element. This applies even if the cash for buying the annuity has come from the lump sum obtained by commuting part of a pension fund.

The amount of the payment from a purchased life annuity that is considered as the tax-free capital element is based on a statutory formula and refers to prescribed mortality tables. It will depend on your age when you take out the annuity. The insurance company will tell you at the outset what the capital element of your annuity is – the older you are, the higher the capital element so the less the tax on your annuity payments.

Alternatively, you may know that you can use the cash payment more profitably by skilful investment, which will more than compensate for the pension forgone.

providing for your dependants

Nearly all personal pension policies offer the option to guarantee that payment of the pension will continue for a specified number of (usually five) years. If you should die within that time, the payments would continue to be made to your spouse or other nominated dependant for the remainder of the guaranteed period. If you take up this option, your own pension will be reduced – perhaps by 4 per cent for a 5-year guaranteed payment for someone retiring at the age of 65, or 10 per cent for guaranteed payment for 10 years.

If you live beyond the guaranteed period, nothing will be paid to your spouse or dependant when you do die.

If a guaranteed element does not form part of the initial contract, the insurance company will probably ask you at the time you reach the retirement age whether you want a guaranteed period of payment and to whom it should be paid if you die within the period.

Some insurance companies offer a widow's or widower's reversionary annuity – that is, a continuing pension to your widowed spouse – also called a 'joint life and survivor annuity'. This can be either the same as the amount you will have been getting (which will be lessened by your taking up this option) or a percentage of your pension.

life insurance
In addition, or alternatively, you can make provision for your dependants by taking out a life insurance policy which will pay out a tax-free lump sum or a series of lump sums to your dependants after your death. (With life insurance, in contrast to an annuity, the age factor has the reverse effect: the older you are when you take out life insurance, the higher the premiums.)

If you qualify for a retirement annuity contract under Inland Revenue rules you also qualify to take out a special type of term or protection-only life insurance. These are known as 'section 226A' policies (because that is the section of the Income and Corporation Taxes Act 1970 under which they can be issued). The important factor with these policies is that the premiums are not liable to tax – they are made out of pre-tax income which means that you get tax relief at your highest rate of tax. (This is especially attractive now that tax relief has been abolished on ordinary life insurance policies taken out since 13 March 1984.)

To get full tax relief, the premiums to any 226A life insurance policy (or policies) must not come to more in any year than 5 per cent of your net relevant earnings; they will count as part of the $17\frac{1}{2}$ per cent limit on how much you can invest in a personal pension scheme each year. So, when keeping a record of premiums paid over the years to any personal pension scheme, in order to know how much unused tax relief you can bring forward from the previous six years, remember to count in any premiums to a 226A life insurance policy.

The premiums are generally relatively low for this type of 'pure' life insurance, which pays out only in the event of death before a specified age: no death, no payment.

A section 226A policy need not be simply a standard policy providing a fixed lump sum should you die within the term of the policy. It can be an increasing term insurance (the later you die, the larger the lump sum) or a decreasing term insurance (the later you die, the smaller the lump sum – but the smaller the premiums throughout).

Or you can take out a term insurance that provides 'family income benefit' in which the equivalent of the lump sum is paid in instalments from the date of your death until the end of the policy term. You can arrange for this to be an escalating benefit so that the amount goes up each year. With some of these policies, the premiums stay the same throughout; with others, they increase in line with the increase in the benefit that would be paid. Choose a policy with which the benefit payable increases from the year after you start the policy rather than one with which the amount increases only after your death.

A section 226A insurance policy taken out since the 1980 Finance Act can be written 'under trust'. This means that, on your death, the sum assured can be paid out straightaway to the nominated beneficiary without having to go into your estate and therefore does not have to be counted in for inheritance tax assessment. All the trustees have to do on your death is to produce a valid death certificate to the insurance company and then payment from the policy can be made without delay.

You do not have to buy a section 226A life insurance policy from the same insurance company as the one(s) with whom you have a personal pension policy. It may be administratively convenient, but the insurance company which offers an attractive pension plan may not be so competitive in life insurance. Some companies, however, do not charge the usual administration fee for issuing a section 226A policy if you already have an approved pension policy with them.

When taking out a policy, you have to decide for how long you want the term of the policy to be. This will probably depend on how near you are to retirement, on your age and that of your dependants. Should you be no longer contributing to a personal pension policy, you would not be allowed to continue with the section 226A insurance.

getting payment

When you reach the age specified in the policy for the pension to become payable, unless you have notified the insurance company (or bank or other approved organisation) that you want to put off drawing on the policy until a later date, you will be told how much your pension will be. This amount will be either what you were expecting from the deferred annuity for which you have been paying premiums over the years or, with a cash-funded scheme, what the sum accrued in the fund from your premiums will now buy you in the form of an immediate annuity. You may then have to make calculations about commuting any part of the money into a cash payment.

tax

The pension that comes from a retirement annuity is liable to tax. (This, to some extent, is where the Inland Revenue get back some of the tax relief allowed on premiums and investments.)

The payments you get from an annuity bought through the pension policy will come from the insurance company net of basic rate tax. A higher rate taxpayer will then have to pay the difference in the tax due by making separate lump sum payments to the Inland Revenue. If you are by then below the basic rate tax threshold, you can ask the insurance company specifically to pay you the gross amount; otherwise, you will have to claim tax refunds periodically from the Inland Revenue.

sources of information

Make sure in good time that you have all the information relevant to your own circumstances, and that you understand all the provisions. The insurance company should be able to help you with any queries you have about the terms of the contract and what pension it should produce. Ask about any choices you may be able to make at this stage to alter the terms of the contract, and the effects of any options.

If you want general information about personal pension schemes or about where to go for individual advice, perhaps about the most suitable type of policy to take out as you near retirement, the following professional bodies should be able to help, and can supply a list of their members in a particular area:

○ The British Insurance Brokers' association
BIBA House, 14 Bevis Marks, London EC3A 7NT (telephone 01-623 9043)
○ The Corporation of Insurance & Financial Advisors
6–7 Leapale Road, Guildford, Surrey GU1 4JX (telephone 0483 39121)
○ The Society of Pension Consultants
Ludgate House, Ludgate Circus, London EC4A 2AB (telephone 01-353 1688)

BIBA publishes a regularly updated *Life & Pensions Brokers Directory* (free) which lists the names of its members who are specifically experienced in this line of business.

Detailed information about different policies, insurance companies' performance, current annuity rates, and so on, is published by specialist magazines, such as *Planned Savings, Money Management, Policy Market, The Savings Market*. These are expensive publications, but copies should be available in a public reference library. Also **Which?** publishes reports from time to time on pensions (state and private) and has regular reports on money matters and investments.

The Superannuation Funds Office, a department of the Inland Revenue, is responsible for seeing that pension schemes meet the rules for approval under relevant tax legislation. The SFO (Lynwood Road, Thames Ditton, Surrey KT7 0DP, telephone 01-398 4242) can be asked about any statutory restrictions or conditions relating to retirement annuity contracts, such as the normal age of retirement for self-employed occupations and the requirements when taking early retirement because of ill health.

proposed changes to pensions

Under the Social Security Act 1986, certain changes will be introduced during the coming decades to pensions from the state, from an employer's scheme, from a personal pension plan.

Most of the changes will scarcely affect anyone retiring within this century.

From November 1986, the criteria for an employer's pension scheme to qualify to contract out of the state earnings-related scheme have become less stringent. Regulations are proposed to allow 'money purchase' schemes to contract out of the state earnings-related pension scheme. For five years up to November 1991, any newly established scheme that contracts out of the state scheme will get a bonus from the government in the form of 2 per cent of the earnings on which employees in the scheme pay national insurance contributions being added to the scheme's fund. Many employers, therefore, may decide to set up a contracted-out scheme, in order to benefit from this incentive.

The requirement that a contracted-out scheme must provide a guaranteed minimum pension (broadly equivalent to what would come from the state earnings-related scheme) is still binding on any contracted-out scheme. But a scheme set up since November 1986 does not have to provide 'requisite benefits' to match state earnings-related pensions (SERPs), as previous schemes do.

From April 1988, a wider choice will be available to employees, who will then be able to opt not to partake in an employer's scheme nor to stay in the state earnings-related scheme but to take out his or her own pension scheme, in much the same way as a self-employed person has always been able to do.

FITNESS AND HEALTH

At any age, people feel better, look better and on the whole are generally healthier if they are not overweight and eat a sensible balanced diet, get adequate sleep and exercise.

A well-balanced mixed diet contains carbohydrates (bread, potatoes, rice), fats (margarine, milk, cheese), protein (meat, eggs, fish), vitamins and minerals in fresh fruit and vegetables.

Wholemeal bread, coarse green vegetables, salads, unpeeled fruit and bran all help to provide fibre in the diet. Vitamin D, which is needed along with calcium to maintain healthy bones, is found in eggs, liver, saltwater fish and is formed in the skin following exposure to sunlight.

If you are used to eating lunch at your office or works canteen, make sure that after retirement you will continue having at least one proper meal each day when you have to provide it yourself. Try not to make up for missed meals by getting through packets of biscuits. Being at home all day you may be tempted to eat more: make sure that you keep an eye on your weight, following your retirement.

If you eat more than your energy expenditure requires, you get fat. Carrying too much weight makes people more liable to develop diabetes and diseases of the heart, and may aggravate arthritis.

The body requires at least three pints of liquid a day so that the kidneys can function effectively. There is no harm in beer or wine, in moderation, but too much alcohol can lead to health problems, quite apart from the other costs.

smoking

Even if you have been a smoker for many years, it is still worth stopping, today. By the time you are fifty or sixty, you are surely aware that smoking is bad for you.

A cigarette smoker runs a much greater risk of lung cancer than non-smokers do; cigarette smoking is not only associated with lung cancer, but also with coronary heart disease and chronic bronchitis.

Smoking reduces the appetite, can blunt the sense of taste and smell, causes bad breath and indigestion, and will alter the normal rhythm of the heart beat. Cigarette smoking, even in moderation, greatly reduces the chances of enjoying a healthy retirement.

There is no easy method of stopping smoking; most people who fail have decided only to 'try to give up smoking' rather than having made a firm decision to stop. Do not expect to succeed unless you have great willpower.

The Consumer Publication *Avoiding heart trouble* explains the risks associated with cigarette smoking, and offers advice on ways of giving up.

sleep

People differ in the amount of sleep they need. By and large, an adult's pattern of sleep is retained until the onset of old age. But there can be temporary upsets due to worry, pain or other physical disturbances.

Sleep is a habit which, if it is broken for whatever reason, can sometimes be difficult to re-establish. Because one of the causes of insomnia is worry and stress, the worry (justified or not) about the approach of retirement, and change of lifestyle associated with retirement, may make a previously sound sleeper develop less regular sleeping habits.

Insomnia is the persistent inability, real or imagined, to sleep. Anyone waking up very early feeling fresh and well has probably had enough sleep and is not suffering from real insomnia. However, people who repeatedly wake in the early hours and feel tired and depressed should consider getting help from their doctor.

People who take little exercise, or sit and doze in an armchair all the evening, should not expect to fall asleep the minute they go to bed and then to sleep all night. It might be a good idea to take a brisk walk before going to bed, as part of a regular bedtime routine. Some people find that a hot milky drink last thing at night will help them sleep, but they should not be misled into believing that special branded bedtime drinks have some particular sleep-giving quality; these have no advantage over any other non-stimulant hot drink. It is the routine that matters and can help people who have difficulty in falling asleep.

the bed

Also, make sure that your bed is comfortable. If you feel stiff when you wake in the morning, it may be for no other reason than that the bed is unsuitable. For good support, and a comfortable night's rest, the mattress should be firm and should not give by more than about two inches at any part. If your mattress is beginning to sag, buy a new one. Mattresses are expensive and it may therefore be a good idea to buy one before retirement, when you still have more money. Good mattresses are best on a firm solid base.

Although some people think that a so-called orthopaedic mattress would be a good investment for their retirement, there is no evidence that such a bed would do more for you than any other firm mattress on a good base.

aches

When you are standing or walking, be aware of your posture. Much back trouble can be prevented if the back and abdominal muscles are kept strong and in good tone and if you avoid stress on the spine, particularly in the region of the lower back. Be careful how you lift and carry heavy things. Your posture when sitting is important, too. A chair should support the small of your back and allow you to sit tall.

If you have persistent backache, or pain or stiffness in the joints, this may be due to arthritis. Consult your doctor.

Too many people attribute unpleasant symptoms to age when, in fact, they may have an illness which can be diagnosed and treated. If you feel unwell or notice that you now need to do things in a markedly different way, do not dismiss such symptoms as mere signs of approaching age.

seeing your doctor

Go and see your doctor about any symptoms that worry you, including

- pain in the chest (sudden or severe or persistent)
- continuous pain in the abdomen
- blood from any part of the body – in urine, in stools (making them look black) in sputum, in vomit
- localised weakness of an arm or leg
- breathlessness
- loss of weight
- hoarseness that persists
- a lump in the breast, in the groin, in the neck – anywhere in the body
- fainting
- persistent irritation of the skin, persistent itching, an ulcer
- unnatural tiredness
- frequent need to urinate
- marked change in bowel habits.

The doctor may be able to recognise a potentially serious disease – diabetes, high blood pressure, heart trouble, cancer – in its early stage, and carry out treatment at a time when it can be effective. He can send you for specialist examination if necessary. Many diseases come on insidiously and can be dealt with or avoided if action is taken in time.

And if there is nothing seriously the matter, the doctor can reassure you and advise you on what you should do to keep yourself in good health. You should never feel guilty about seeming to waste the doctor's time. There is no reason why you should think that you must put up with pain or discomfort, just because you are getting older. Middle age – or old age – is not an illness.

The Open University runs two courses, called *Look after yourelf* and *Health and retirement*, intended for group discussion. They are sold in sets of six for £24 each. Single-person packs are also available for £8 each course. For further information contact the Learning Materials Service Office, The Open University, POB 188, Milton Keynes MK7 6DH.

regular check-ups

Neglect in middle age can quite unnecessarily lead to losing your teeth. Make a regular dental appointment every six months, even if your mouth seems healthy, but particularly if you show signs of bleeding, bad breath or loose teeth. You should go to a dentist who is prepared to take trouble with your gums and to give your teeth regular scaling. If you have dentures, get them checked every three years.

Most people need glasses for reading as they grow older. If you are finding it increasingly difficult to read or to see things near you, go and have your eyes tested. You do not need a doctor's referral: just make an appointment under the national health service with an ophthalmic optician or an ophthalmic medical practitioner. Regular eye examinations are important not only to get a prescription for reading glasses but also because diseases can be detected, such as glaucoma which can creep up on people without their being aware. If, in the course of a routine sight test, any suspicious signs are found, you will be referred to your general practitioner who may send you to a specialist in the hospital eye service.

private health insurance

There are private medical centres in London and some other cities, such as Nottingham and Manchester, where you can have a health screening test (for a fee of around £200; slightly reduced fee for members of the private health insurance responsible for the particular centre).

The older you are at the time of joining a private health insurance scheme, the higher the annual premium. The upper age limit for taking out private health insurance is generally 65 years but there are some special schemes for older people.

exercise and sport

There will be more time for exercise and sports after retirement. If you have been in the habit of taking regular exercise, carry on – if you have not done anything physically active for many years and never thought of doing so, do so now. There is no need to feel that you are too old, or too flabby, or likely to make a fool of yourself. However, do not suddenly take up a new form of strenuous exercise and

o do not take undue exercise when you are not feeling well or recovering from influenza or a bad cold
o if you are not used to sports, start with only short periods of exercise and gradually and regularly increase the time and vigour
o never ignore fatigue; take a rest when you are tired
o avoid exercising to the point of severe breathlessness, pain or distress.

some suggestions

Walk, cycle, swim as much as possible, and keep going with any sport you have been doing. If you want to take up a suitable new one, the choice includes badminton, bowls, golf, table tennis, dancing (country and ballroom), keep-fit. A form of exercise particularly suitable for people as they grow older is a chinese form of keep-fit called Tai Chi Chuan which is a pattern of movements designed to keep all the limbs flexible. It is a kind of gentle, contemplative dancing. Classes are held at adult education centres, and other places, and once you have learned the movements, you can carry on by yourself.

The Sports Council has a series of '50+' leaflets with suggestions for out-and-about activities (such as hiking, rambling, orienteering, bird watching); for 'sports centre activities', including their likely costs and the equipment needed; on 'lending a hand', with suggestions for participating in the activities of a local sports club. These leaflets should be available at your local library.

When you are retired, you will be in a position to use sports facilities during the less crowded parts of the week, such as public tennis courts at three o'clock on a tuesday – the time when you used to be at your desk – and the swimming pool at ten in the morning.

Swimming is not only very healthy, at any age, but has the advantage that you do not have to rely on finding a partner or a team. On the other hand, there is an advantage in taking up, or continuing, a sport that allows (or even forces) you to meet others.

A good first contact is your local sports centre or the recreation department of the local authority. The regional office of the Sports Council (headquarters at 16 Upper Woburn Place, London WC1H 0QP, telephone 01-388 1277) will also be able to help with suggestions and local addresses.

learning to enjoy leisure

Even a person who has been looking forward to retirement as an opportunity to expand his or her interests and develop a new lifestyle will need a period of adjustment after perhaps 45 years of regular employment. When suddenly there are no deadlines to be met, no regular journeys to get to work, no need to leave the home at a specific time every day, and the whole day is yours, you may wonder what to do with all this freedom.

Being free does not mean being idle. Leisure can be used for doing things out of interest rather than for money, doing what you have always wanted to do – including pottering around, gossiping, reading with your feet up and relaxing.

Perhaps there will be a different slant to leisure. If, during your working life, you led a very sociable life, it may have been a relief to get away on your own. In retirement, however, you may feel the need for company of like-minded people and therefore decide to join an association, club or group – which is a good thing for someone who has no longer the usual everyday contact with fellow workers.

There are groups and associations for most leisure activities, and being one of a group also imposes some discipline: if the weather is bad, you are more likely to go out for a game of golf if it has been arranged with others, than force yourself to go out for a walk alone. When free time is unlimited, you may need to exert more self-discipline than you would have imagined, in order to do even the things you most enjoy.

classes

While working, many people start courses or evening classes – but fall by the wayside. Many of these classes may be on offer during the day, under the auspices of the local education authority. The Workers' Education Association (Temple House, 9 Upper Berkeley Street, London W1H 8BY) also offers a varied selection of day time and evening classes. There is no reason why a retired person should not continue to go to evening classes, nightschool, adult education courses.

The National Extension College (18 Brooklands Avenue, Cambridge CB2 2HN) offers 10 per cent discount on home-study courses to members of the Pre Retirement Association.

The University of the Third Age (U3A) promotes self-help educational activities – run, taught and attended by retired people who are encouraged to contribute their own particular skills, knowledge and experience, and to learn from those of other members. For information about local groups, contact the Executive Secretary, U3A, at 6 Parkside Gardens, London SW19 5EY.

trying new activities

Some colleges and community centres provide facilities for people to experiment with several hobbies or activities before committing themselves to buying equipment and paying course fees. In some centres, the skilled members teach each other various crafts (and thus course fees are kept to a minimum).

Here is a short list of hobbies you may not have thought of, but may want to give a try:

brass rubbing, calligraphy, car maintenance, cooking, copper/pewter work, corndolly craft, dressmaking, embroidery, jewellery making, lampshade making, leathercraft, macramé, marquetry, painting, pottery, sketching, soft furnishing, weaving, woodwork.

Despite cuts in education budgets, if there is a demand for a particular type of class, most authorities will do their best to try to meet it. Classes may include: astronomy, comparative religions, creative writing, genealogy, languages, musical appreciation, philosophy, public speaking, yoga. The cost of classes varies from area to area, but there may be some reduction for retired people.

It may be possible to join an amateur dramatic or an amateur operatic society, not necessarily as the leading tenor or even to take a walk-on part, but helping behind the scenes, to make props, to sew costumes, to be the 'resident electrician', to sell programmes on the night.

People usually take up a hobby for their own pleasure but may find that in retirement they have more time to share it with others. The model railway enthusiast will easily find many enthusiastic youngsters to share his interest, and there is always an audience for anyone who has studied local history and local architecture.

Remember that it is more important to enjoy the activity than to achieve perfection. If you are hesitant about speaking in front of people, take a public speaking course. However, be realistic. Not many people are going to change drastically in late middle age. While inside every shy retiring mouse there may be an extrovert lion trying to get out, if that has not happened by the age of 58, it is unlikely to happen after a public speaking course at 62 or 68. Or if you have 'always wanted to write novels' but never found the time to put pen to paper, it is unlikely that you will turn into a Jane Austen at 61.

being prepared through pre-retirement courses

Many companies think that it is not their responsibility to prepare their staff for retirement. But in fairness to some employers who do, employees are often reluctant to attend pre-retirement courses, perhaps because they do not want to think about, or plan for, their own retirement (maybe they think that, like accidents, it is something that happens to other people).

A pre-retirement course might cover sessions on the following subjects:

○ pensions (occupational and state)
○ reduced income, wills, tax changes
○ health: keeping fit, exercise, nutrition
○ leisure, work, voluntary work
○ housing, moving, making your house more convenient
○ concessions: travel and other, and how to find out.

If your firm does not provide a pre-retirement course, bring the matter to the attention of the personnel department, the staff association, your trade union branch.

The Pre Retirement Association, 19 Undine Street, London SW17 8PP (telephone 01-767 3225) may be able to give you advice on what courses are available in your area. The Association is mainly concerned with encouraging pre-retirement education. The majority of members are companies, but private individuals can join; generally they join their local, affiliated, organisation. There are some forty local Pre Retirement Associations (in some localities known as Pre Retirement Council or Retirement Association, or Pre Retirement Committee). They include GLAP (Greater London Association for Pre Retirement) and PRAGMA (Pre Retirement Association of Greater Manchester) and may be county-wide or concentrate on a single locality. You can find out the address of your nearest Pre Retirement organisation from the PRA headquarters in London.

Choice, the monthly magazine of the Pre Retirement Association, available from newsagents at 80p, gives advice on a variety of topics, including health, housing and finance.

The Open University runs a course called *Planning retirement* which invites people approaching retirement to examine their own experience and expectations in making realistic decisions for the future. The course consists of a study pack costing £20 and an (optional) assessment pack costing £10, available from the Learning Materials Service office, POB 188, Milton Keynes MK7 6DH.

Preparation for retirement is obviously concerned with hard practical matters – finance, housing, health. It should also help to prepare you for more leisure, and deal with family and emotional relationships and how the change in routine will affect you in your new life.

DOMESTIC ADJUSTMENTS

Where the husband's and the wife's relative ages are such that he retires while the wife is still working full-time, the situation can produce special stresses. A man may be lonely and feel neglected while his wife is still working, especially if his own retirement is unwelcome. He may therefore need considerable emotional support. On a strictly practical level, it may be worth sitting down together and deciding who does what in the new regime. The man might have to learn to contribute more to the practical running of the home, now that he spends more time there. There may even be a small lesson there for a man who could not understand what the wife did all day long . . .! However, it is unlikely that a man who has never ironed his own shirts (let alone anyone else's), will suddenly want to do so now, or find great fulfilment in doing such tasks. But vacuuming, dusting, shopping are jobs that do not require a long apprenticeship.

A man may have been holding down a responsible job for years, but not know how to cope with finding himself alone in the house with a shopping list and set of instructions for the family meal. Start preparing him gently, now. Some men are excellent cooks. He should be encouraged to watch a tv cookery course, or attend a cookery course at the local tech, or adult education centre. Some run special courses just for men.

There may be a sudden realisation that everybody else seems to be pursuing their own goals, including the children who may now be offering advice to their father in his new role. All these situations of role-reversal call for tact and understanding on everybody's part, and it may take time to adjust.

Message to wife at retirement stage: can you mend a fuse, fill in a tax form, mow the lawn and mend the lawnmower, do the decorating, turn off the mains water? Get him to teach you now – he may not be around forever. And vice versa.

women

Some of the effects of retirement are different for women than men, whether they are themselves retiring, or living with a man who is about to retire.

Where the man has retired and the wife does not go out to work, it can mean less freedom for her. A non-working wife who is used to her own routine may find it difficult to adjust to having someone around all the time. She has her own friends, her hobbies, her own way of life. Perhaps she is used to a snack lunch (or none at all) and now is expected to produce a cooked meal every midday.

The need for understanding and adaptation within the family is vital. Men may find it difficult to adjust to being around the house all day, too. In this situation, both parties need to use tact and understanding to adjust gradually to their new situation.

In retirement, most couples will be seeing more of each other than ever before in their married life, so what may have been a minor irritation, because they were not spending so much time together, might become a source of real friction. You may decide to grin-and-bear it; or, by putting words to a problem, it may turn out to be something trivial, after all. If it unleashes thirty years' bottled-up resentment, that, too, may be a good thing if it helps to clear the air.

It is not always appreciated that a woman's retirement from work affects her just as a man's does his. Women who resumed work after having a family or looking after a relative may particularly miss the companionship and interests outside the home, and the mental stimulation, which a job provides. A man may assume that housework will provide his wife with something to do, to fill the gap after retirement, but forgets that one of the reasons why many women go out to work is to prevent their housework expanding into a full-time job. She may not relish a return to a life dominated by household chores.

single people

Anyone living alone may particularly miss the companionship of colleagues at work, and there may be a feeling of isolation to cope with, as well as adjustment to a life no longer centred round work. But the actual pattern of domestic life may not be all that much disrupted and, for a gregarious person, the change may not be very dramatic.

If you are single or widowed and faced with living alone in your retirement, you may need to make a special effort to get involved with your neighbours and invite friends or acquaintances home –

not necessarily for a meal, but perhaps for coffee or, now that afternoons are free, for tea.

Offer your services as a babysitter and you may become the most sought-after person in the street. Perhaps do some shopping for someone who is housebound. Try to keep in contact with all age groups and, particularly, avoid falling into the trap of separating yourself from young people, even if you are mutually suspicious. If you have any expertise to offer or experience to share with young people, explore ways of becoming involved in helping them. But do not approach them on a senior-to-junior level: that is a recipe for disaster.

Consider inviting a student to live with you, as a paying, or non-paying guest. Contact the accommodation officer at your nearest college or university or teaching hospital. Tell him or her the type of student you would prefer: male or female, young or mature, for example, so that you will get somebody who would not be disruptive to your way of life. Many young people and mature students are serious and conscientious, some are lonely, especially overseas students. With a bit of give-and-take, the advantages (including the financial contribution) could outweigh the disadvantages, and may in fact work out extremely well for all concerned. If not, you can always opt out of it next term.

putting affairs in order

Some people have their affairs in order all the time, but for those who have not, the run-up to retirement or perhaps immediately after having retired, when you have more time on your hands, is a good opportunity to sit down and take stock. For people who are planning to move house, there may be a need to sort things out, to throw out old papers and clobber and be forced to get themselves well and truly organised.

Both partners should know where important documents are kept, insurance policy for house, car, life insurance, deeds to property, share certificates, and so on. A person living alone who, in an emergency, would be dependent on neighbours, should have placed in some obvious position the telephone number and address of a close friend or relative who could be contacted.

have you made a will?

Making a will does not mean that you are going to die one minute earlier; not making a will may well mean that your possessions, after death, will go to someone to whom in life you would not have given them. You may think that it will all go to your wife/husband anyway, but he/she may die before you. Whether it will all automatically go to the spouse depends on how much the 'all' is, and whether there are any surviving children, or possibly surviving parents. The Consumer Publication *Wills and probate* sets out clearly what happens to the possessions of a person who dies intestate (that is, without having made a will) and describes what is involved in making a will.

considering inheritance tax

One important matter to bear in mind when making a will is that inheritance tax (IHT) affects transfers of property on death, that is gifts, legacies and bequests, and certain transfers within seven years before the date of death. However, there are some exemptions from IHT; the most relevant of them is that each year a person can give away £3,000 without tax; that on death, no IHT is payable on (at present) £71,000, and that all property passing from husband to wife (or vice versa) on death is wholly exempt from inheritance tax. This is an advantage if you plan to leave it all to your wife/husband. But bear in mind that tax will then have to be paid when she or he dies. So it is worth considering, all other things being equal, to make a will that uses up the £71,000 tax-free allowance in favour of, say, children.

appointing executors

It is usual to appoint executors, in a will. An executor is the person whose responsibility it will be to see that the wishes expressed in the will are carried out. To do so, the executor of a will has to obtain a grant of probate (which involves a certain amount of paperwork and calculations), pay the IHT (not out of his own pocket, but he has to make the arrangements for the payment), pay off the debts of the person who has died, and make sure everything is perfectly in order, before distributing the property to the people who are to benefit from the wishes expressed in the will (the beneficiaries). It is therefore a responsible, time-consuming job, even when everything is quite straightforward. Often two people are appointed to be executors, to share the burden. It is a good idea to appoint as executors one or more of the main beneficiaries who have a stake in seeing that the administration is carried out as smoothly as possible.

Although it is not binding on the person who is named in a will to act as executor when the time comes, it is best to ask first, before making the appointment, so as to give the person a chance to say 'no' and to let somebody else be appointed.

Instructions for my next-of-kin and executors, available from Age Concern England (Bernard Sunley House, 60 Pitcairn Road, Mitcham, Surrey CR4 3LL, price 25p) is a useful 4-page form on which to fill in detailed personal financial information that will help executors when the time comes for them to act.

As one grows older, it is inevitable that certain friends and relatives will die. There is no need to avoid discussion of the subject. For instance, if someone you care for feels strongly about, say, cremation or formal rites, it is right that you should know – and vice versa.

power of attorney

Many people at retirement age have elderly relatives who may be finding it increasingly difficult to look after their own affairs. It may be advisable to get a power of attorney for them.

A power of attorney is a document which gives one person authority to act on behalf of another. It need not necessarily be used immediately, perhaps never. The elderly relatives should continue to be in charge of their own affairs as they were before. But in the event of, perhaps, a stroke or something which prevents them from writing or dealing with official papers or the bank, for instance, the power of attorney is there to be used.

Until 1986, the ability of one person to deal with another's affairs under a power of attorney was limited by several factors. First, a separate power of attorney was needed for dealing with a person's own personal affairs and dealing with his affairs as trustee. The trust power of attorney was limited to twelve months.

Even a general power of attorney became revoked as soon as the donor ceased to have the full mental capacity which would have been necessary to sign the relevant document himself. The only way of dealing with such a person's affairs was the extremely complicated and expensive method of appointing a receiver through the Court of Protection.

the difference now

Under the Enduring Powers of Attorney Act 1985, it is now possible for a donor (that is, the person giving power of attorney to someone else) to execute a power of attorney both for trust and for other matters, and with a view that the power of attorney should 'endure' through any intervening incapacity of the donor. This can therefore obviate the need for the appointment of a receiver through the Court of Protection.

The enduring power of attorney must be executed by the donor and donee on the designated form, obtainable through law stationers. Until any incapacity, it will operate in the same way as a general or trust power of attorney would have operated. Should the donor then become incapacitated, the power of attorney ceases in the same way as it used to. However, the difference is that the power of attorney can now be resurrected without application through the Court of Protection simply by registration in the Court of Protection, after certain formalities have been strictly complied with.

All the forms required must be in the official form obtainable through law stationers. The power of attorney itself must be executed by the donee as well as the donor in the presence of a witness who must then add his signature, name and address and occupation.

It is possible to limit the power of attorney in any way the donor sees fit but unless any limitation is placed on the attorney's power in the document, the donor should realise that the donee can use the power of attorney for any purpose – including the making of gifts to himself or herself.

on incapacity

As soon as the donee has reason to believe that the donor is, or is becoming, mentally incapable he must make an application for registration of the power of attorney in the Court of Protection. Before doing so, notice must be given to prescribed degrees of relatives of the donor. The order is as follows:

> Spouse, children, parents, brothers and sisters (of the whole or half blood), widow or widower of a child of the donor, grandchildren, the children of the donor's brothers and sisters of the whole blood, the children of the donor's brothers and sisters of the half blood, the donor's uncles and aunts and, finally, the children of the donor's uncles and aunts.

Notice has to be given to every person in each of the above groups, in order, until three persons have been so notified provided that all the members of the particular class are notified, even if that means giving notice to more than three persons. A person is not entitled to receive notice if his name and address is not known or cannot reasonably be ascertained by the donor, or if the attorney has reason to believe that such person has not attained the age of 18 or is mentally incapable. The attorney need not give notice to himself or to any other attorney who is joining in making the application for registration. Notice must also be given to the donor. The period of notice is four weeks. The grounds of objection to the application are specified in the notice.

After that, the application for registration (again in the statutory prescribed form) can be made to the Court of Protection when the period of notice has expired without any objection having been received. A fee (£30) is payable for lodging the application with the Court of Protection.

The requirements as to notice and forms must be strictly adhered to: there will probably still be a short period, of up to six weeks or so, when the registration formalities are being gone through, during which the attorney should not use the power of attorney.

Once the power has been registered, the attorney may proceed to use the power of attorney as before and can sign letters of instruction on behalf of the donor, deal with any matters relating to any bank account of the donor and sign any documents relating to sales of stocks and shares and land.

getting advice

In all situations where you may need explanations about official documents, or need help and advice generally on any official or legal or administrative matter, or want to ask questions about pensions, the local citizens advice bureau might be able to help.

If necessary, you can find out the address of your nearest citizens advice bureau by getting in touch with the registry department of NACAB, Myddleton House, 115 Pentonville Road, London NI 9LZ (telephone: 01-833 2181).

help in making ends meet

You may think that you are too well-off to qualify for any help, but if you find it difficult to make ends meet, make sure you know what you are entitled to, by checking with your local social security office or the social services department at your town hall.

Anyone below retirement age not working full-time whose income is below a certain statutory minimum, with savings of less than – at present – £3,000 can apply for supplementary benefit, designed to meet ordinary living expenses. Leaflet SB1, available from social security offices and post offices, gives full details and a claim form.

People getting supplementary benefit normally have their rent and rates met in full. Others on a low income may be entitled to claim housing benefit; the amount depends on the size of the family, and the amount of rent or rates payable. Application has to be made to the housing department of the local authority, on form RR1 which you can get from the local social security office.

family income supplement

A lone parent in paid employment for at least 24 hours a week, or a couple where one partner works at least 30 hours per week, whose income is below a certain statutory minimum and has at least one child living at home who is under the age of 16 (or over 16 but under 19 and still at school) can apply for family income supplement (FIS). Leaflet FIS1, available from social security offices and post offices, gives full details and a claim form.

Children are the qualifying factor, but someone forced to retire at, say, 58 may well still have a school-age child, particularly of a second marriage.

future changes

There are current government proposals for replacing supplementary benefit with an income support scheme, and replacing family income supplement with a family credit scheme, to take effect from April 1988.

the telephone

Telephone payments can be spread over the year by buying telephone stamps at the post office at regular intervals, or through a monthly direct debit based on average usage.

If you have a rented phone and make few calls, you may be able to take advantage of the low user rental rebate. On lines rented at the residential rate, where the number of call units per quarter is less than 120, a rebate of 3.6p is given for each unused unit below 120.

supplementary pension

A person over the state retirement age, who is not in paid full-time work, and whose resources are less than his or her requirements (both according to official definitions), may qualify for a supplementary pension in addition to any state retirement pension. It is a non-contributory pension, that is, not dependent in any way on the number of NI contributions a person has made. To be eligible, the gross income (less various allowable expenses) must be less than a set figure, which depends on whether you are a single person or a married couple, and on some other factors. The supplementary pension is not taxable.

Leaflet SB1, available from local social security offices or post offices, gives details and a claim form.

You will have to give particulars of all your income, and other detailed information, in a personal interview with someone from the social security office. You can choose to have this interview in your own home rather than at the social security office.

Anyone in receipt of a supplementary pension is automatically entitled to other benefits, for instance, help with heating costs in certain conditions.

If you have a low income or claim supplementary pension, you may be able to claim help with fares to and from hospital. Get leaflet H11 for further information.

Someone getting a supplementary pension who needs glasses

will get a voucher to use in payment for the spectacles, and so may someone with an income only just above supplementary benefit level. Leaflet A11 explains vouchers for glasses.

Dental treatment is free if you are receiving supplementary pension (make sure you tell your dentist, and ask him for form F1D); you may also qualify for free treatment or help with charges if your income is low.

WORKING AFTER RETIREMENT

If you have retired early, before qualifying for the state retirement pension, you may need to supplement your income by finding some paid work. This may not be easy because you will be competing against much younger people, but some employers may prefer an older person.

Some firms agree to employees 'slowing down' before they retire – working, say, four days a week in the last year or two. Others are willing to let people continue on a part-time basis after they retire (doctors doing one clinic a week, for example). Even where someone has retired early because the job has dwindled, there may still be opportunities with the firm on a self-employed, freelance basis.

If there is no scope for you there, or if you want a complete change of scene, start looking as soon as you know that you will be prematurely retired. Use the old-boy network, use your connections through pub and club, church, old business contacts: if you do not tell people that you are available, they will not know, or be aware of the fact that you are looking for a job. Tell your relations, neighbours, friends, acquaintances. And, of course, go to your local jobcentre.

Use any trade or professional institutes and societies of which you may be a member; use your trade union.

Do not forget the Professional Executive Register (PER), established by the Manpower Services Commission, or the employment agencies that specialise in particular trades, industries, professions. Find out about, and approach, local self-help groups and local centres for the unemployed run by the TUC and MSC. They tend to concentrate on younger people, but may provide opportunities for someone near retirement age.

The search may be long and tedious. You are more likely to achieve success if you present yourself well, and have a carefully prepared curriculum vitae. But you may have to be willing to take a job in a new field and may need to retrain.

retraining

A reason for having to take early retirement may be that technology has outstripped your own knowledge and experience. So, for a new career or new occupation, consider retraining.

You can approach the Job Training Scheme (through your local jobcentre) and see what is available for you, at your age, and whether – and on what conditions – they will take you on. One condition is that you must be willing to take up employment in the occupation for which you train, but there is no guarantee of a job.

Examine what courses are on offer at your local adult education centre or technical college; the library is a good place to look for information and announcements. While looking for retraining courses, you may come across other courses or lectures that may be useful.

co-operatives
In recent years there has been a revival in small co-operatives. A co-operative is a business venture jointly owned by the people who work in it, conducted on business lines, but distributing any profits amongst its members on a democratic basis.

A co-operative may be set up under the Companies Act with a minimum of two people, or under the Industrial and Provident Societies Act with a minimum of seven people. You, too, could get together with other people and start your own co-operative. An example would be a small local gardening service with two or more people gardening and others providing back-up in book-keeping, enquiries, maintenance.

Further information, and a publications list, can be obtained from the Co-operative Development Agency, Broadmead House, 21 Panton Street, London SW1Y 4DR (telephone: 01-839 2988).

How to set up a cooperative is amongst the information included in the Consumer Publication *Starting your own business*.

possible placement agencies

Some employment agencies which specialise in placing older people include:

Executive Stand-By Ltd, at 310 Chester Road, Hartford, Northwich CW8 2AB and *Executive Standby (South) Ltd*, at office 51, London Wool Exchange, Brushfield Street, London E1, and *Executive Standby (West) Ltd*, at Somercourt, Homefield Road, Saltford,

Bristol BS18 3EG, have a register of executives who are available to fill short-term, and long-term, consultancy vacancies.

Intex Executives (UK) Ltd, Chancery House, 53–64 Chancery Lane, London WC2A 1QU provides senior executives or managers to employers, on a short-term basis.

Success After Sixty, 40–41 Old Bond Street, London W1X 3AF is an employment agency which will introduce to employers people over 50 who are looking for part-time or full-time employment.

Buretire (UK) Ltd, run by The Employment Fellowship, Willowthorpe, High Street, Stanstead Abbotts, Herts SG12 8AS, is an employment bureau which aims to find part-time employment for retired and disabled people.

The Emeritus Register is a scheme to link retired former employees of a number of large firms, who are still keen to work, with businesses and organisations seeking part-time or short-term help. It covers both voluntary and paid employment.

Only pensioners of firms who are in the scheme can participate; it is up to firms to join the scheme for the benefit of their own future ex-employee pensioners. Employers who are interested should get in touch with the administrator of the scheme at 8 Quadrant Arcade, Romford RM1 3EH.

earnings rule

If you are past retirement age, remember the 'earnings rule': you lose 5p of basic pension for every 10p you earn over £75 a week up to £79, and 5p for every 5p (that is, pound for pound) earned over £79. (These figures are periodically updated.) And anything you earn may affect the amount of tax you have to pay. So you may find that to make it worthwhile, you would have to earn a high salary or fee, perhaps higher than you can demand. Your earnings count for the week in which they are earned, even if you do not receive them until later. If you do not know in advance how much you will earn, your pension may be reduced in line with an estimate of what your earnings might be, and will then be adjusted when the final amount is known. It is always worth checking beforehand to see if and how your pension will be affected.

A person who has retired may want to find work not just for financial reasons but for personal ones, such as getting out of the house, companionship, involvement.

occasional jobs, freelance work

Even in today's economic climate there are employers who may be glad of someone who is willing to work for, say, two or three hours a day, or one day a week, perhaps saturdays (cinema queue-marshall; checking weekly holiday makers in and out of hired accommodation; doing workshop repairs for a store) earning just within the limit. There are seasonal jobs for a retired accountant to prepare small firms' books, for an ex-civil servant to advise on form-filling; someone to man the office when all the workmen (boss included) are out on jobs; a handy-man to do an accumulation of repairs in, or decorate the outside of, a house, or do odd-job gardening.

Employers know how much a retired person can earn without his or her pension being affected. The remuneration can often be tailored to fit the pensioner's free limits, but beware of being exploited. It may be tempting to accept cash-in-hand payment, but it is probably better to insist on the rate for the job and be ready to pay tax on it.

In today's economy, it may be difficult to obtain even part-time employment on a reasonable salary, but it is quite possible that voluntary or 'expenses-only' work can be found – possibly more than one job. Voluntary jobs, although not offering a salary or pay, may cover travelling expenses (and give you the opportunity to travel – even if it is only to the other end of town), and expenses such as post and telephone calls.

Telephone calls, even if they are strictly for business purposes, mean that you have to be in communication with outsiders: a defence against the isolation that some people fear in retirement.

voluntary work

Many people do voluntary work in a limited way without really considering it as voluntary work – that is, by helping neighbours in the community. After retirement, with more leisure, it is possible to do so in a somewhat more organised way. In some respects, voluntary work can offer some of the bonuses that employment gave you: company, outside involvement, a sense of personal value and an up-to-date reference, which should be particularly useful if you decide to try a part-time return to paid work in the future.

There are many voluntary organisations, and in every sphere there is always demand for volunteers, not only for the large national organisations, but in local ones – for example, local housing organisations, local hospital, local Oxfam shop. The Employment Fellowship runs activity centres to enable people to use their skills and maintain contact with other people. They always need volunteers. For details of your nearest centre, contact the Employment Fellowship at Drayton House, Gordon Street, London WC1H 0BE (telephone: 01-387 1828).

To find voluntary work, you might also start by contacting your local authority's social services department regarding

○ meals on wheels
○ visiting the house-bound
○ visiting the hospital-bound
○ hosting at an old people's club
○ assisting the youth officer at a young people's club
○ preservation of public footpaths (may come under the technical services department of the local authority)

The public library may have information about local societies (or you might start a group, if there is none) concerned with environment matters, pollution of air, soil and streams; disappearance of hedges; threatened closure of branch railway line or rural bus service.

Contact the National Trust (head office at Queen Anne's Gate, London SW1 9HS, telephone: 01-222 9251) about helping, on a rota basis, to man and look after Trust properties in your area.

Retired Executive Action Clearing House (REACH), 89 Southwark Street, London SE1 0HD (telephone: 01-928 0452) links retired executives to useful work with voluntary organisations on an expenses-only basis.

Many councils of social services run voluntary workers' bureaux which are designed along the lines of an employment exchange.

In paid employment, people usually have some idea of the hours they will work, the type of work they would like to do and the money they would like to earn. Some of the same considerations apply to voluntary work, so be prepared to ask about them at any voluntary workers' bureau. Make sure that if you are going to do voluntary work you will not be out of pocket: if you are offering your services free, do not hesitate to ask if your expenses will be covered.

enjoy it

Many of us have to spend our working life doing jobs we are not particularly keen on because we need the money, but this is not a consideration with voluntary work in retirement. Every voluntary organisation has a wide variety of jobs on offer, and skills needed. Think what skills you have to offer (and want to offer) before deciding to contact any organisation.

Do something which you are going to enjoy because there is little point in doing voluntary work unless you are going to get some satisfaction from it. If the smell of hospitals makes you feel upset or uneasy, there is no point in going to do voluntary work in a hospital. If you do not care for children, then working with them would be a mistake. If you are put on 'fund raising' and find this is uncongenial, ask for an alternative job – say office work or something within the scope of your capabilities which you will be happy and comfortable doing.

If you have been dissatisfied with the job you have been doing for the last ten or twenty or more years, and been eagerly awaiting the opportunity of retirement, think carefully before going back to doing the same thing – but without the pay.

An important consideration before offering yourself for voluntary work is how much time you really want to give. When you have quite a lot of free time, you may want to be very generous with it. But voluntary work snowballs: if you have not had any experience of it, a good idea is to offer a couple of hours to begin with, and then do more if you enjoy it and find that it is not going to encroach too much on your freedom. Sometimes volunteers deal with people who become very dependent, so that it is difficult to resist demands – until the 'two hours' develops into four or more.

On the other hand, we all like to feel that we are needed and voluntary work can give a great deal of satisfaction.

help exchanges

Exchanging help for help is not a new concept and good neighbours have been doing it since time immemorial.

Often people who do not fall into any particular category of great need would like a little help from time to time – with the garden, income tax returns, redecorating, shortening the sleeves of a jacket, seeing what is wrong with the car – and yet are unable to pay much (or anything) for it because they are retired and living on a limited income. It would only take a few retired people living in the same area to set up a bank of skills, offering one hour of a skill in exchange for an hour of any other skill. Self-help groups need not be restricted to retired people. An exchange of skill on a time basis could extend to every member in a community and all age groups.

CONCESSIONS

some
things
you
can do
cheaply

Once you reach state retirement age (65 or 60) you will qualify for a number of concessions and benefits. For some, you need proof of age, and perhaps proof that you are a resident of the area; for others, you have to be able to produce your pension book.

Someone having the pension paid directly into the bank, should ask the local social security office for form BR 464, so that a card giving proof of retirement age can be sent from the Department of Health and Social Security; this card can be used instead of a pension book to obtain concessions.

travel

Most local bus companies, both those run by the local authority and privately run ones, let senior citizens travel either free or at reduced rates. There may be restrictions, such as no concessionary travel during certain hours; or extra bonuses, such as allowing a companion to travel free or at reduced rates at weekends.

Find out what the situation is in your area, from the local bus company; a bus conductor may be a good first contact. National Express reduce their inter-city coach fares by one-third for senior citizens.

trains

The British Rail senior citizen railcard is available to everyone over 60 and costs £12 for one year. The card entitles you to various reductions in fares. At present these are:

○ one-third discount on off-peak monthly returns ('saver tickets')
○ one-third discount on standard single tickets
○ one-third discount on standard return tickets
○ one-half cheap day-returns (off-peak day-returns)
○ half price standard day-returns.

You can take four children aged under 16 with you, for a set price per head each. There is also a discount on Sealink British Ferries and Torbay Seaways. For travel on inter-city sleeper services you have to pay the full sleeper supplement but only the discounted fare.

Holders of a senior citizen railcard qualify for a discount when travelling as accompanying passenger on certain Intercity Motorail services.

You can also buy a £7 card which entitles you to off-peak day-return tickets at half price. With this, too, you can take up to four children with you under the same conditions as for the £12 card. They do not have to be your own grandchildren or other relatives, so this is an opportunity to take a neighbour's or a friend's children on an outing.

At present, a senior citizen railcard also entitles you to reduced travel on the London underground (but this may cease after May 1987).

There are certain restrictions about trains on which the concessionary fares do not apply. British Rail have leaflets which give up-to-date information.

air travel

A reduction of 30 per cent on the full normal round-trip fare for any flights within the UK is available on British Airways. The return journey must not be until six days after the outward flight.

foreign rail travel

Many of the European railway companies offer reductions to their own senior citizens, some extend these to foreign travellers.

A British Rail senior citizen railcard entitles you to buy, for £5, a Rail Europ senior citizen railcard which gives savings on the cost of travel from the UK to 17 continental countries and on journeys within those countries, namely

- 50 per cent reduction on railways in Belgium, Finland, France, Eire, Greece, Holland, Luxembourg, Norway, Portugal, Spain, Sweden, Switzerland
- 30 per cent in Austria, Denmark, Hungary, Italy, West Germany, Yugoslavia
- 30 per cent on sea crossings by Sealink, Hoverspeed and Townsend Thoresen, when the crossing is part of a rail/sea through journey to points in Europe.

The main restriction on the use of a Rail Europ card is on travel which starts in one of the foreign countries during parts of the weekend. But if you start your journey in this country and travel through to your destination without any stopover, the fares reductions do apply even for weekend travel.

holidays

In retirement, life might seem one long holiday, but even so it is important to think of getting away from home, if only for the odd day, for the stimulation of seeing and doing different things and having a complete break from the usual routine.

Some tour operators specialise in holidays for older people, which usually means over 55 years of age. The Greater London Association for Pre Retirement has compiled an information sheet (No. 7 holidays) which gives details; your local Pre Retirement Association may produce a similar information leaflet.

Most of these holidays are for out-of-season periods.

leisure activities

Some theatres offer reductions for matinees or some mid-week evening performances, usually one ticket per person – so if you go with someone below retirement age, you may sit side-by-side for different prices.

Local authority concessions will vary from area to area, but might include reduced entrance to swimming baths at off-peak times of day; waived fines on overdue library books; museums, stately homes, art galleries and exhibitions that normally charge an entrance fee may waive or reduce it. Such clubs and associations offer membership at a reduced fee or allow non-members above retirement age to buy tickets (such as the National Film Theatre in London). Many ordinary cinemas offer seats at half-price for their afternoon performances. The admission fee for some sports events may be reduced.

Even private businesses, such as dry cleaners and hairdressers, may offer reductions.

All this varies from place to place, so you will have to keep your eyes open for notices and, if in doubt, ask if there is an OAP reduction.

NHS concessions

When you reach the official state retirement age, prescriptions are free. Just tick the box on the back of the prescription form and fill in the details in the space provided.

INVESTMENTS

You can leave thinking about investment for retirement until the day you actually retire. But to make the most of your money, decisions have to be made not just at the time you retire but in the years leading up to retirement.

When you have worked out how much income you will have when you retire, you may realise that it may be wise to try and spend less money now and invest it, so that you can have more later, when you have retired.

Saving can be done on a regular basis in an organised scheme, or in an ad hoc manner, putting aside odds and ends as you get them. But do not just put the money aside, invest it.

Even if you are not familiar with investing money, you may find that now you have to make decisions about it.

planning ten years or so before retirement

If you have around ten years before you retire, you could consider a long term savings scheme – perhaps one with a greater element of risk than if you leave it till later. But do not start such a scheme unless you can keep up with the payments. Remember that the money will be tied up for ten years (or the period you agreed to save for). It is not wise to enter into a long-term financial commitment shortly before retirement. Some ways of saving are:

○ unit trust savings schemes: these can produce high growth, but can be risky because the value of the money you invested can go down instead of up
○ life insurance savings schemes (usually for a minimum of ten years), assuming your health is reasonable: these include with-profits endowment policies, and unit-linked life insurance (which is a somewhat less steady way of saving, because the value of the money can go down as well as up)
○ National Savings Certificates: these give an unexciting return, except for higher-rate taxpayers, but are very safe
○ British Government stocks: from these you get a guaranteed return; start looking around now for new issues of stocks maturing when you are likely to need the money back
○ index-linked investments: from these the return may not be high, but it is guaranteed to keep pace with inflation.

planning four or five years before retirement

One way of saving which may be particularly good in the last few years before retirement is by making additional voluntary contributions to your pension scheme. It depends on your own particular pension scheme how good an investment this will be for you.

Since you only have a comparatively short period to save for, you should stick to the safer forms of investment. These include:

○ National Savings investments
○ building society and bank investments
○ British Government stocks
○ index-linked investments.

planning a year or so before retirement

Your choice of saving methods is now much more limited. You may still be able to make additional voluntary contributions to your pension scheme. Otherwise stick to the safest form of investment, such as National Savings investments or building society or bank investments.

planning when you retire

As you come up to retirement, you should be planning how you will use or invest any lump sums you may get. These could come from several sources:

○ many pension schemes pay out, or give you the choice of, a tax-free lump sum in place of part of your pension
○ you may have got a lump sum from selling your house and moving to a cheaper one, or from the sale of your car.

You may have accumulated a lump sum from saving and investments made over the last few years (for example, a life insurance policy which is due to mature on retirement). But you should be careful about when you cash in or start to draw income from these investments. It may not be the best time to realise such a lump sum, because of the state of the market. And to draw an income when you do not really need it may affect your tax bill.

You may decide to 'invest' part of a lump sum on enriching your retirement, for example, getting a really good workshop or garden, buying a hi-fi, or going on the holiday you could never before afford. Or you could spend part in ways which will save you money later on, for example, a new washing machine, a more reliable car, a fuel-saving central heating system.

But the odds are that you will still need to put something aside, to provide an income later on. To someone retiring with a lump sum, it may be the first large sum of money he or she has ever had. That is exciting, and also alarming, so do not be tempted simply to put it all into the building society, without considering all the options.

You can, of course, ask for advice from investment advisers such as a bank manager, insurance broker, accountant. But remember that advisers may have a vested interest in where you put your money – because they can get commission from all sorts of organisations, such as insurance companies or unit trusts. Or they may be under pressure to sell their own products, for example a bank may have its own range of unit trusts. So their advice may not be as unbiased as you think. In general, you should try to find out about investments and make your own decisions: it is your money, so you should care more than anyone else.

how investments differ

Investments can differ in several ways: the return they give and how it is paid; how they keep their value; when you can get your money back; the tax position; how safe they are.

the return
What you get back from an investment can come in two different forms, income or growth. Firstly, you might get an income paid out to you in the form of interest or dividends. Secondly, with some investments, you expect (or hope) that the value of the money you invested will grow and give you a capital gain.

In practice, these two different forms of return can overlap. In some cases, you can add the income to the money you have already invested (this is sometimes called rolling-up the income), so that the value of the investment will rise. You can also cash bits of any capital gain, to give yourself an income.

how the return is paid

There is generally some regularity in the way investment income will reach you – every month on a certain day, or quarterly, or at longer intervals. It can be inconvenient if the money is only paid out annually, and you depend on it for a monthly income. Annual payment can also mean that you get a lower rate of return than you think. That is because if you have the use of the money sooner you have the possibility of re-investing it and getting interest on that too, so that the return from the investment will be compounded.

the value of the money you invest

Even if it stays the same in £££'s, the purchasing power of each £ invested will be eroded by inflation. For instance, if inflation is running at ten per cent a year, and you are getting a return of nine per cent from your investment, you will be losing out because the value of the money invested, plus the return, will buy less at the end of the year than at the beginning. To avoid this happening, you can choose index-linked investments which guarantee to keep pace with inflation.

With some investments, the value of the money you invested stays the same, and the return comes solely in the form of income – as for example, a building society account.

With other investments, the value of the money you have invested can go up and down – as for example, a unit trust. This is riskier, because if the value goes down you lose money; on the other hand, you hope that it will go up to give you a capital gain and help to protect your savings against inflation.

when you can get your money back

With some investments, you cannot get your money back until the end of an agreed period; an example is an income bond, where you agree to invest your money with a life insurance company for a period usually between two and ten years. With some other investments, such as a building society or bank 'notice' account, you agree to give a period of notice (for example, one week or three months) and can get your money out at the end of the period of notice.

In many cases, you can get your money out of an investment earlier than the agreed time – for example by surrendering a life insurance policy early, or by giving up interest on a building society account. But if you do this, you can end up getting less out of the investment than you put in. So if in any doubt about when you will need the money, keep at least some in an investment where you do not lose out if you withdraw the money early, even if it means a slightly lower return.

Some investments have no time restrictions but the value rises and falls. So if the value is low when you want to cash the investment, it may be prudent to wait for a suitable moment to get your money back.

tax

Different levels and ways of taxing can make one investment very good for a higher-rate taxpayer, unattractive for a low taxpayer, and so on. The most suitable investments for higher-rate tax-payers are usually tax-free ones, or those where the return comes mainly in the form of a capital gain rather than income (because the highest rate of tax on capital gains, if you have to pay any at all, is 30 per cent whereas the highest rate of tax on income is 60 per cent).

Non-taxpayers should also be careful how the income from an investment is paid. Most investments are now paid with basic rate tax, or its equivalent, already deducted before you get the income. With some investments, people who should pay no tax can reclaim the tax already deducted. But with more and more investments – which include most building society, bank and finance company accounts, and loans to local authorities – the tax cannot be reclaimed, however low your income. Non-taxpayers should only choose these investments if the return, even after tax, is still better than on other investments available.

○ savings accounts with a bank, building society or finance company
○ index-linked investments which guarantee to keep pace with inflation.

funds for boosting your income now
Investments which will give you an income now or in a short while include:

○ an annuity
○ interest-paying accounts with banks, building societies, finance companies
○ local authority investments
○ National Savings investment accounts and Income bonds
○ life insurance company income bonds which pay out a fixed income for a number of years
○ National Savings certificates (you can cash these in at regular intervals to provide an income).

funds for boosting your income later
You may anticipate needing more income after, say, ten years of retirement, because of likely changes in your circumstances. But even if you think you are likely to need the same income as time goes on, it is still prudent to ensure that you can draw an increasing income, because of the effect of inflation.

You can do this by investing at least some of your money in an index-linked investment, such as index-linked National Savings certificates, or index-linked British Government stocks. Another way is to invest part of your lump sum for growth, rather than income, to try to get an increase in its value. Then in perhaps five or ten years, if you find that you need to boost your income, you could cash this investment and use it to provide more income. Suitable investments for this include:

○ unit trusts which aim for capital growth (these will pay out very low incomes)
○ shares
○ investment trusts
○ single premium investment bonds.

building up a portfolio

It is unlikely that just one investment is going to suit all your needs. So once you have decided what these needs are, you may have to build up a portfolio of investments. This allows you to include some safe investments to guarantee at least a minimum of income as well as more risky investments which give you the chance of a capital gain, investments where you can get your money back easily in an emergency, as well as ones which offer a better return at the cost of having to leave your money tied up for some time. But when building up a portfolio, remember:

- investments which offer the chance of a capital gain also have the chance of a capital loss; so, balance these more risky investments with safe ones
- many investments have a minimum sum you can invest, which may limit your choices: if you cannot afford to spread your money among many types of investments, choose safer investments rather than risky ones
- find out about tax before investing
- find out how the return is paid, and compare the true annual rate of return or compounded annual rate of interest (CAR) with that of others (with many types of investments such as in building societies, banks, CAR is advertised, so you can make a comparison)
- keep some money in an emergency fund
- do not tie up all your money in long-term investments: your circumstances may change unexpectedly
- if an investment offers what seems like an exceptionally high return, proceed with care – it may do so at the cost of high risk, too.

tax on investments

The two types of tax which affect investments are income tax and capital gains tax.

income tax

Some types of investment income are tax-free, but most types are taxable. Taxable investment income is added to your earned income and taxed in the normal way.

The tax on taxable investment income is gathered by the Inland Revenue in one of three ways. With a few types of investments, the income is paid out with no tax deducted; anybody who has to pay tax on this income, then pays it either in their tax bill or through Pay As You Earn on their job or pension.

Other types of investment pay out an income after basic rate tax has been deducted. If you are non-taxpayer, even after this income is taken into account, or should pay less tax than has been deducted, you can claim tax back. If you are a higher-rate taxpayer you will have to pay extra tax.

But more and more types of investment nowadays deduct the equivalent of basic rate tax, at a special composite rate (fixed at 25.25% for the 1986–87 tax year), before paying out an income. Even non-taxpayers cannot reclaim this tax, and higher rate taxpayers have to pay more. To work out the before-tax amount of this type of income (the gross amount), you have to 'gross up' the interest you get, by dividing it by 0.71 per cent. For example, if the interest payments you get in a tax year amount to £335, the grossed-up amount of interest is £355 ÷ 0.71 = £500.

So, when choosing an investment, you have to take into account how the income is taxed. Non-taxpayers should beware of investments where they cannot reclaim tax, unless the return even after tax is better than that from other investments. They should also remember that even if they can reclaim tax, they may have to wait for some time until their rebate arrives. Higher-rate taxpayers should consider putting their money into tax-free investments, or investments which are taxed as capital gains rather than income.

age allowance

If you are retired you pay tax like anyone else. But if you are over 64 by the start of the tax year (or if you are a married man and your wife is) you can claim the higher age allowance (in the 1986–87 tax year £2,850 or £4,505 if married) instead of the normal personal allowance.

However, once what is called your 'total income' reaches a certain amount (£9,400 in the 1986–87 tax year) your age allowance is reduced rather sharply. For every £3 by which your 'total income' exceeds the (£9,400) limit, you lose £2 of your age allowance, until the allowance is reduced to the level of the normal personal allowance. It can never be reduced to less than this amount. (In the 1986–87 tax year, your age allowance is reduced to the level of the normal personal allowance if your 'total income' is £10,173 if single, £10,675 if married.)

To work out your 'total income', add up your gross income for the tax year. Include:

○ the grossed-up amount of any interest from which the equivalent of any basic rate tax has been deducted before you get it, for example building society or bank interest
○ any taxable gain on a life insurance policy
○ both husband's and wife's incomes.

Then deduct:

○ interest you pay which qualifies for tax relief (for example, interest on a mortgage to buy or improve your home)
○ contributions you pay to an employer's pension scheme or personal pension plan
○ half the amount of any Class 4 national insurance contributions you pay
○ the gross amount of any covenant payments and enforceable maintenance payments you make.

how to save your age allowance

If your income is so high that each extra £ of taxable income loses you some age allowance, extra care may be necessary when choosing your investments.

Consider putting some of your money into tax-free investments. After the saving of tax and age allowance is taken into account, the return may be better than that for an investment with a higher rate of return at face value.

Be careful about cashing in all or part of a life insurance policy on which you will make a taxable gain. Although there is no basic rate tax to pay on such a gain, it will be included in your 'total income' and so could reduce your age allowance. If you pay tax at higher rates and you cash in a life insurance policy or make it paid-up within its first 10 years (or within the first three-quarters of its term if that is shorter) you will make a taxable gain.

Consider an annuity, if one would suit your needs in other ways. Provided that you buy the annuity voluntarily, with your own money and not as part of your pension scheme, only part of the income is taxable and counts towards your 'total income'.

claiming income tax back

If you have investment income from which basic rate tax is deducted before you get it (but not composite rate tax), and you are a non-taxpayer or your tax bill should be less than the amount of tax deducted, you should claim a rebate. With dividends from shares and most unit trust distributions, the payments will be accompanied by a tax voucher showing that you get a tax credit. If your tax bill comes to less than the total of tax deducted plus tax credits received, you will have paid too much tax and should also claim a tax rebate.

If the Inland Revenue think you can claim a rebate, you may well get a special *Tax claim form R40* instead of the normal kind of tax return. You should fill it in and send it back with the tax vouchers you get with the income. You do not need to wait until the end of the tax year to do this: claim as soon as you have received all your relevant investment income for the tax year.

The taxman will work out how much tax you are owed, if any, and send you a rebate. Arrangements can be made for repayment of tax by instalments during the year; ask your tax office for details.

If you have to claim tax back regularly, but are not sent form R40 automatically, ask your tax office for it.

capital gains tax

You may make a capital gain whenever you part with something for more than you paid for it. However, most people are unlikely to have to worry about capital gains tax on their investments, because:

o some investments are tax-free altogether
o your capital gain is reduced by an indexation allowance; this prevents you being taxed on any gain made purely as a result of inflation
o capital losses you make are deducted from capital gains in any tax year; this reduces the amount on which you pay tax
o a certain amount of chargeable capital gains you make is free of tax (in the 1986–87 tax year this is the first £6,300).

If you do have to pay capital gains tax, it is due at a single rate of 30 per cent.

Capital gains made on the following types of investment are tax-free:

o the sale of your only or main home (if you have more than one home, you can choose which one you want to count as your main home; it does not have to be the one you live in most of the time)
o investments passed from husband to wife, or vice versa
o National Savings certificates and Yearly Plan
o premium bond prizes
o proceeds from life insurance policies, unless you bought the policy from a previous holder
o British Government stocks
o the sale of personal belongings, antiques, jewellery, and other moveable objects, provided the value of each object when you sell it is £3,000 or less.

which type of investment?

Here is a brief outline of the main types (in alphabetical order, not in order of priority).

annuities

You can buy an annuity for a lump sum from a life insurance company and it gives you a guaranteed income for a set number of years – usually until you die.

The older you are when you buy the income, the higher your annual income. Women usually get less than men of the same age, because their life expectancy is longer. For example, in return for £10,000 invested in February 1987, a 65-year old man who paid tax at the basic rate could have got an after-tax income of about £1,215 a year for life: a 75-year old woman could have got £1,396.

Couples can buy annuities which carry on paying out until the last one of the couple dies. These are known as **joint life and survivor annuities**. The income is lower than for a single person the same age as the older of the two people.

Most companies give you a choice of how often the payments are made, annually, quarterly, monthly. If they are made more frequently than once a year, each is lower, so this will mean a slightly lower income in total.

There are many different types of annuity. You can get ones where the income starts lower than with a 'level' one but gradually increases over the years. For example, assuming an annuity which increases by 5 per cent a year, it will take some six or seven years for an increasing annuity to pay the same income as a level one and will then continue increasing your income steadily.

You can also get what are known as **deferred annuities**. With these, the income only starts some time after you made the payment – five years, say. By buying in advance, you get a higher income when the payments actually start. But this type of annuity does involve some risk. Because the income available from an annuity varies from time to time in line with interest rates in general, you may find that you bought your annuity at a bad time.

With the basic type of annuity, the income stops when you die, irrespective of how soon after buying the annuity that may be. But some types of annuity are either **guaranteed** – where the payments continue for a set number of years even if you die – or **protected** – where your family get a lump sum back if you die within a set time. You get a lower income with this type of annuity.

You can now also buy **with-profits** and **unit-linked** annuities. With these, the purchase money is invested in with-profits or unit-linked investment funds. This means that you get a slightly lower income to start with, but if the funds in which the money is invested do well, you may get an increased income later from investment bonuses and increases in the value of the units, which will help protect your income against inflation.

Current rates of annuities are shown in trade magazines such as *Planned Savings*, *Money Management*, and *Savings Market* (which you will find in your local reference library). If you decide to buy, check with the insurance company first that the rate you have seen is still being offered.

tax:
Part of the income from an annuity is treated as return of some of the lump sum you paid, and this part is tax free. The other part is treated as interest on your lump sum, and this is taxed as investment income. Basic rate tax is usually deducted before you get it. Non taxpayers can ask to have the income paid without this deduction; higher rate taxpayers will have to pay some extra tax. With an annuity which you buy as part of a personal pension plan, the whole payment is treated as earned income.

pros and cons:
The payments are guaranteed. But although annuity rates vary, you continue to receive the rate that applied when you bought your annuity. So you will do well or badly, depending on how interest rates change after you buy the annuity. And unless you

choose an increasing annuity, or one linked to a with-profits or unit-linked fund, the purchasing power may be eaten away by inflation. An annuity is basically a gamble. With most types, if you die, however soon after buying one, your family gets nothing back (and paying for a protected or guaranteed annuity means a lower income). You may be willing to put up with these risks for the sake of a guaranteed income. But the income available at younger ages means it is not worth buying an annuity below the age of 70, at least.

bank investments

The high street banks now offer a large and varied range of investments, many of which are very similar to those offered by building societies and finance companies. With many accounts nowadays, the more you have invested, the higher the interest rate. Many banks offer facilities such as cash machine cards on some of their savings accounts.

Bank deposit accounts have the advantage that the minimum you can invest is generally very low, usually as little as £1. But the interest rate is usually low too, and the equivalent of basic rate tax is deducted before you get it. Even non-taxpayers cannot reclaim this tax. In theory, with most deposit accounts you have to give seven days' notice if you want to get your money out. In practice, the bank will pay out on the spot, but some banks deduct seven days' interest. Some banks now offer cash machine cards on deposit accounts. Interest is worked out on a daily basis and is usually added to your account twice or four times a year.

Higher rate deposit accounts: in return for a higher minimum investment of, say, £1,000, you get a higher interest rate than for an ordinary deposit account, and can get your money out at once.

High interest cheque accounts: these offer some banking facilities, such as cheque books and standing orders, and also a higher interest rate than for an ordinary account. You can get your money back on demand, but there is usually a high minimum investment, of around £1,000 upwards.

Fixed notice or penalty accounts: when you invest your money, you agree to give a fixed period of notice, say 28 days, before you cash it in. In return, you get a higher interest rate than for an ordinary deposit account. You may be able to get your money back at once, by losing interest. The minimum investment varies, but may be around £1,000.

Fixed term accounts are still offered by some banks. You invest for a set period of time – say, one, two, three or six months – and cannot withdraw the money earlier. They differ from other bank investments in that the rate of interest may be fixed at the time you open the account, and will not change even if rates change during your investment. This gives you the certainty of a fixed income, but whether or not it proves to be the best return will depend on how rates change after you invest. The minimum investment can vary from several hundred to many thousands of pounds.

Regular savings accounts: a few banks offer regular savings accounts where you agree to save a set amount – for example £10 a month. Whether or not you can withdraw the money varies from bank to bank.

tax:
Since 6 April 1985 most bank interest has been taxed in the same way as building society interest – that is, the equivalent of basic rate tax is deducted before you get it. This tax cannot be reclaimed, and higher rate taxpayers will have to pay extra tax.

pros and cons:
The income from bank investments is generally variable and, because it comes in the form of interest rather than capital gain, has little protection against inflation. This also means that banks can be a secure place to keep money. The great variety of bank accounts now means that you may be able to find rates of interest as good as those offered by building societies. Roughly speaking, the more money you have to invest, the higher the interest rate – although you can also get a higher interest rate if you are prepared to tie your money up for some time. Some bank saving accounts

also offer the convenience of banking facilities such as cheque books and cash machine cards. Non-taxpayers should remember that they cannot reclaim the tax deducted from the interest.

British Government stocks

The government issues these (also known as gilt-edged securities, commonly shortened to 'gilts') as a way of borrowing money.

The prices of gilts are quoted as the price for each £100 of nominal stock. When gilts are first issued, you pay £100 for each £100 of nominal stock you get, and the government promises to redeem them at face value at a set date, which can be as distant as 2024 or as close as 1988 (though a few gilts are undated and have no set maturity date). In the mean time, the holder gets a set amount of interest, usually twice a year.

You can buy gilts when first issued, and hang on to them until maturity, which makes them a safe way of getting a set income from a lump sum. Alternatively, you can buy them after they have first been issued or sell them before they are redeemed, on the Stock Exchange. If you do this, the price can vary – it can be above the nominal value or below. Roughly speaking, the price of gilts falls if interest rates in general rise, and vice versa. So you can also use them as a speculative way of investing, and make a capital gain (or loss) when you sell them, depending on the price at which you buy and sell.

You can also get **index-linked gilts**. If you hold the stock from when it is issued until it is redeemed, it is guaranteed to keep pace with inflation. At redemption, it is worth the face value of the stock, increased in line with inflation over the lifetime of the stock.

So the return from British Government stocks can come in one of three forms:

○ a regular income (normally fixed). Some stocks, known as 'high coupon' stocks, pay out a high income; 'low coupon' stocks pay you a low income so are more attractive to higher rate taxpayers or people who do not want a high income but are more interested in making a capital gain

○ a capital gain or loss if you buy the stock after it is issued or sell it before it is redeemed
○ with index-linked stocks kept to redemption, guaranteed protection against inflation.

You can buy and sell either through a stockbroker, bank or other investment adviser, in which case you will probably have to pay commission. Otherwise you can, for certain gilts only, buy through the National Savings Stock Register, commission-free. You can get more details about, and an application form for, this Register from your local post office. When there is a new issue of British Government stock, you can buy direct by filling in a coupon from newspapers such as the *Financial Times*, the *Guardian*, the *Independent*, *The Times* and the *Daily Telegraph*.

tax
Interest is taxable, but is paid before deduction of tax if the stock is bought through the National Savings Stock Register. Otherwise, basic rate tax is normally deducted before you get the interest. Non-taxpayers may be able to reclaim this tax, higher-rate taxpayers will have to pay more. Any capital gain you make on selling is free of tax.

pros and cons
British Government stocks are a versatile investment which can be used either to provide a safe and regular income for a fixed period, or as a more risky way of making a capital gain (or loss). They are not a suitable home for money you might need in a hurry. If interest rates go down generally, to below the interest rate of your gilts, you could do very well both because you continue to get a comparatively high income, and because the price of the stock would be high if you sold. The reverse could apply if interest rates go up. You can also use index-linked stocks to guard against inflation.

building society investments

There is now a great variety of building society accounts, and you can get a better interest rate by being prepared to shop around. A magazine such as *Building Society Choice* (from MoneyGuide, Riverside House, Rattlesden, Bury St Edmunds, Suffolk IP30 0SF can help you choose. Many building societies now offer some banking facilities too, such as cheque books, cash machine cards, and standing orders. Although the names given to accounts vary from society to society, they fall into some basic types:

Ordinary share accounts: these have a low minimum investment – usually £1 – so can be a good place for saving odds and ends of money. You can get your money back at once, although the amount you can draw in cash without notice may be limited (to £250 in cash, say, £5,000 by cheque). **Deposit accounts** are very similar to share accounts but pay a slightly lower rate of interest because they are deemed to be slightly safer.

Fixed notice or penalty shares: when you invest your money, you agree to give a fixed period of notice, say 28 days, before you cash it in. In return, you get a higher interest rate than for an ordinary deposit account. You may be able to get your money back at once, by losing interest. The minimum investment varies, but may be from around £250 upwards.

High interest, no notice shares: these work exactly as the name suggests, but there is usually a higher minimum investment than for ordinary shares. The more you can invest, the higher the interest rate.

Subscription share accounts are suitable for saving a regular sum of money – say £10 a month. These accounts vary widely from society to society; there are usually restrictions on when you can withdraw the money.

Monthly income accounts are offered by some building societies, often as variations on their normal accounts. You may have to make a bigger initial investment to qualify.

With most building society accounts, the interest will vary with interest rates in general. But you can occasionally find building society accounts where the interest rate is fixed at the time you take it out. Such accounts are normally only available for a short period.

On most accounts, interest is credited to the account twice yearly, and with some monthly, which then increases the income considerably. But with some, interest is added only once a year. This can affect the true rate of return from the account, so that an account crediting the income only once a year may offer a lower return than one with the same nominal interest rate which credits the interest twice yearly.

tax
There is no basic rate tax to pay on the interest you get from a building society investment because the equivalent of basic rate tax is deducted at source. If you are a non-taxpayer, you cannot claim back the deducted tax. If you are a higher rate taxpayer, you will have to pay extra tax on the grossed-up income.

pros and cons
The income from building society accounts is generally variable and, because it comes in the form of interest rather than capital gain, has no protection against inflation. But you cannot make a capital loss. They are comparatively safe: there is an Investor Protection Fund which means that if your society goes bust you will get back 90 per cent of the first £10,000 you invested.

You can get a good interest rate by shopping around – particularly if you have around £1,000 or more to invest. You are not married to your building society: if another one offers a better deal, you can withdraw your investments (unless they are on fixed notice), and place them where the interest rates are higher.

Some building society accounts also offer the convenience of banking facilities such as cheque books and cash machine cards. (But non-taxpayers should remember that they cannot reclaim the tax deducted from the interest.)

finance company investments

The savings accounts offered by finance companies vary greatly from company to company. Some offer accounts very similar to those offered by the High Street banks, and facilities such as cheque books, cash machine cards and so on. Accounts offered by finance houses include:

deposit accounts
You usually have to tie up your money for some time and give notice before withdrawing your money: the notice period can range from one month to a year. The minimum investment is likely to be from around £500 upwards.

money market accounts (sometimes called money funds)
In return for a high minimum investment, which can be anything from £1,000 to £10,000, you get a high interest rate (which varies from time to time). You can get your money back at once or by giving a few days notice.

safety
Make sure you invest your money only with a licensed deposit-taker, who will be licensed by the Bank of England and have to meet certain requirements. There is a Deposit Protection Fund, which will pay out 75 per cent of the first £10,000 you have invested if the deposit-taker were to fail. It is not worth leaving the protection of UK laws for the extra money you may get by investing in a deposit-taker which is not licensed (it would have to be based outside the UK, which could mean the Isle of Man or Jersey).

tax
Interest from finance company deposits is taxed in the same way as building society and bank interest. The equivalent of basic rate tax is deducted from the interest before it is paid. Even people who should not pay tax will not be able to reclaim this tax; higher

rate taxpayers will have to pay higher rate tax on the grossed-up amount of the income.

pros and cons

A great variety of accounts is now available. But there is no protection against inflation, because there is no chance of making a capital gain. These investments may not be suitable for non-taxpayers, unless even the after-tax rate of return is higher than they could get elsewhere.

income bonds

This sort of investment is offered by life insurance companies. You invest a lump sum – usually a minimum of around £1,000 upwards – for a set period of time, which can be between one and ten years. During that time you get a guaranteed income, a percentage of the investment. At the end of the period, but not usually before, you get your original investment back.

tax

The tax treatment depends on how the bond works. There is no basic rate tax to pay (the company takes care of this) and with some types of bond non-taxpayers may be able to reclaim tax. Check carefully with the company, before investing that the proceeds from the bond will not affect your age allowance (the special tax allowance for people who are 64 or over at the start of the tax year).

pros and cons

Income bonds offer no protection from inflation, and can affect your age allowance. But they give the security of a fixed income for an agreed period.

investment trusts

Investment trusts are public limited companies quoted on the Stock Exchange. They differ from other companies in that instead of owning buildings or machinery, or manufacturing goods, they exist purely to buy and sell shares in other companies. So buying shares in an investment trust company is a way of spreading your money over a number of companies' shares.

You get a return in the form of dividends from the investment trust company, usually paid out twice yearly. In addition, there is also the chance that you will get more for the shares when you sell than the amount you paid (and vice versa). So you could make a capital gain (or loss) as well.

You buy shares in an investment trust company in exactly the same way as shares in any other company – through a stockbroker, bank, or other investment adviser. You will probably have to pay commission on the purchase. There is, in theory, no minimum investment, although in practice the level of commissions means that it is probably not worth buying less than £700-worth or so of shares.

tax

Investment trusts are taxed in the same way as other companies. The company deducts basic rate income tax from the dividends before paying them to the shareholders. Non-taxpayers can reclaim this tax; higher rate taxpayers will have to pay more income tax. If you make a capital gain, you may also have to pay capital gains tax on the profit.

pros and cons

Investment trusts, like unit trusts, offer you the possibility of a capital gain to protect your income against inflation – but also the risk of a capital loss. So do not consider them unless you can afford to lose the money, and do not put all your money into investment trusts. But if you are prepared to take some risk, they are a sensible alternative to investing in shares directly, because they spread a comparatively small amount of money over a number of companies.

life insurance savings schemes, unit-linked

These are a way of making regular payments into a life insurance fund, which buy you shares (units) in the fund. The value of your units goes up or down in line with the investment performance of the fund. Your plan usually lasts for a set number of years (often ten) after which you have the option of cashing in your units or holding on to them. Some of your payments also go to pay for life insurance: if you die while the plan is running, your estate will get a lump sum; how much depends on your age, state of health, and type of scheme.

You can cash in the plan at any time, but you may get back less than you invested for two reasons:

○ the value of the units can go down as well as up
○ the insurance company makes annual charges which can be high, particularly in the early years of the plan.

Because of this, you should only consider one of these schemes if you are prepared to carry on investing for ten years or so. You can surrender your plan early, but because the company recoups most of its cost early on, the amount you get back may be very low.

The minimum you can invest varies; it can be anything from £5 a month upwards.

tax
The lump sum you get from the plan on maturity or death is free of basic rate tax (the insurance company is deemed to have already paid on its investments). Higher rate taxpayers may have to pay higher rate tax if you cash in the policy in its first ten years, or in the first three-quarters of the time it was planned to last for, if shorter. The proceeds at the end of the term are free of capital gains tax (unless – which is rare – you bought the policy from a previous holder).

If you took out a policy before 14 March 1984 you may be getting a 15 per cent tax subsidy on the premiums. You may lose this subsidy if you alter the policy so as to increase the benefits.

pros and cons

If you are prepared to treat them as a long-term investment, unit-linked life insurance schemes can be a way of making a capital gain (or a capital loss). If you are not prepared to tie your money up for long enough, consider unit trusts or investment trusts instead. Charges can be heavy in the first few years of the scheme. Because prices of the units can go up and down, be careful when you cash in. If all you want is life insurance, other policies are more suitable.

life insurance savings schemes with-profits

You pay regular amounts to a life insurance company which invests your money in a fund. In return, the company guarantees to pay a set amount at the end of the scheme, or if you die while it is running. You also get regular bonuses added to this guaranteed amount. The amount of the bonus depends on how the investments in the fund are doing. The company may also pay a terminal bonus when the policy matures. In recent years, these terminal bonuses have been very high, but there is no guarantee that they will continue to be so, or even that you get one at all.

The minimum you can invest is usually from £5 a month upwards, and the minimum length of time for which such policies run is usually ten years. You may be able to cash it in earlier, but because the company recoups most of its costs in the early years, the amount you get back may be very small, or even less than the amount paid in, particularly in the first five years of the policy.

tax

The lump sum you get from the plan is free of basic rate tax. If you are a higher rate taxpayer you may have to pay higher rate tax if you cash in the policy in its first ten years, or in the first three-quarters of the time it was planned to last for, if shorter. The proceeds are free of capital gains tax unless you bought the policy from a previous holder.

If you took out a policy before 14 March 1984 you may be getting a 15 per cent tax subsidy on the premiums. You may lose this subsidy if you alter the policy so as to increase the benefits.

pros and cons
With-profits endowment policies give a steady return, with the chance of beating inflation. Your family also gets a lump sum if you die while the policy is running (though if all you want is life insurance, this is not the best kind of policy). Once added to the policy, bonuses cannot be taken away, so this sort of life insurance is slightly less risky than a unit-linked life insurance plan. On the other hand, the life insurance company may need to keep some of the investment profits from a with-profits fund back for a rainy day, while with a unit-linked policy more of the profits are likely to be passed on. A with-profits saving scheme should be treated as a long term investment.

local authority investments

There are three main sorts of investments:
    Loans to local authorities: these last for a fixed term, usually between one and seven years. The local authority pays interest on the loan – the amount is fixed when you take out the loan. Once you have invested the money, you cannot usually get it back until the end of the agreed period. The minimum investment is generally £1,000.
    Local authority stock is rather like British Government stock. When it is first issued it can be bought direct from the local authority. After that, it can be bought or sold on the Stock Exchange, and the price goes up or down. So you could make a capital gain (or a capital loss). Alternatively, you could hang on to the stock until it matures, when you will get the face value of the stock. There is no minimum investment in theory, but because of the costs of buying and selling, the minimum sensible investment is around £700.

Yearling bonds work in a similar way to local authority stock, but usually last for a short time, most commonly one year.

You can get information on local authority investments from CIPFA Sterling, 65 London Wall, London EC2M 5TU (telephone 01-638 6361).

tax

Interest on loans to local authorities is taxed in the same way as bank and building society interest. The equivalent of basic rate tax is deducted before you get it, and cannot be reclaimed, even by non-taxpayers. Higher rate taxpayers have to pay extra tax.

The income from local authority stocks and yearling bonds has had basic rate tax deducted before you get it, and higher rate taxpayers have to pay extra tax on it. But non-taxpayers can reclaim tax if their tax bill, including the income, is less than the tax deducted.

There may be capital gains tax to pay on local authority stocks or yearling bonds.

pros and cons

Loans to local authorities have the advantage of offering a set income for a fixed period. But they provide no protection against inflation, and you cannot get your money back before the fixed period is up. Non-taxpayers should remember that they cannot deduct tax from the interest.

Local authority stocks and yearling bonds, on the other hand, do offer the chance of a capital gain to guard against inflation – providing you are happy to take the risk of making a capital loss instead. The price may also be low when you want to cash them in.

National Savings investments

You can either buy or get information about all National Savings investments at most post offices. You can also get up-to-date information by telephoning 01-605 9461. National Savings investments include:

National Savings Ordinary Account: this gives a low rate of interest – guaranteed to be 3 per cent in 1987. But for each whole calendar month in which you keep £500 or more in the account, the interest rate rises to 6 per cent. Interest is added on 31 December, for the preceding calendar year. An Ordinary Account may be attractive to a higher rate taxpayer, because the first £70 of interest a year is free of tax. The minimum investment is £1, and you can withdraw up to £100 on demand.

National Savings Investment Account: this pays a higher rate of interest than the Ordinary one (currently 11.75 per cent before tax), and the minimum investment is only £5. But you have to give one month's notice to withdraw money. Interest is credited to accounts on 31 December each year.

National Savings certificates (32nd issue available in February 1987): you get a guaranteed interest rate, which increases the longer you keep it (but you cannot withdraw the interest unless you cash in a certificate). You get the full advertised return (the equivalent of 8.75 per cent a year on the 32nd issue) only if you hold the certificates until the end of a set period, normally five years. You can cash in certificates before this for a lower return – the repayment value of the certificate increases at the end of the first year, then at the end of each three months. If you cash in during the first year, you get back only the original purchase price of the certificate. You can keep your certificates for longer than five years, when you will get the *general extension rate* of interest, which varies from time to time (at present it is 8.7%).

The cost of each certificate is £25, and the maximum holding of the 32rd issue is £5,000. If you cash in a certificate, your repayment will take some time to come through – it is put in the post within eight working days of your application being received.

Index-linked National savings certificates (4th issue available in February 1987): like other National Savings certificates, you get a guaranteed rate of return, which increases the longer you keep the certificate (up till the end of a set period, currently five years, after which you get the general extension rate of interest). The interest rate is quite low (an overall return of 4.04 per cent a year for the 4th issue), but the Certificates also guarantee that their value is index-linked in line with inflation. If you cash during the first year, you only get back what you originally paid. If you cash in after that, you get back the value of the certificate increased in line with inflation, plus interest.

The minimum and maximum investment, and the way you cash them in, are the same as for other National Savings certificates.

National Savings income bonds in return for a minimum investment of £2,000, you get a monthly income (currently at 12.25 per cent before tax, but the rate can change). You can cash in bonds in multiples of £1,000, provided that you leave £2,000 invested, but you have to give three months' notice. If you cash in during the first year, you get only half the interest rate from the date of purchase to the date of repayment on the amount repaid.

National Savings indexed income bonds: in return for a minimum investment of £5,000 these pay out a monthly income guaranteed to rise with inflation. For the first year the before-tax interest rate is currently 8 per cent (a compounded rate of 8.3 per cent). At the end of every 12 months, the interest is increased in line with the retail prices index. So if prices increase by five per cent in the first year, say, the interest rate for the second year is increased by five per cent to a compounded rate of 8.7 per cent. The bond lasts for ten years, but you can cash it in with three months' notice (interest is halved if you do so in the first year).

The drawback to these bonds is that only the interest is index-linked, not the original investment, so your capital is not protected against inflation. And 7 per cent inflation over 10 years would reduce the buying power of £5,000 to £2,542.

National Savings investments compared

investment	period to get maximum return	notice of withdrawal	minimum investment	maximum investment	return fixed or variable
TAX-FREE					
NS certificates 32nd issue	5 years	8 working days	£25	£5,000	fixed for 5 years
Index-linked NS certificates 4th issue	5 years	8 working days	£25	£5,000	depends on rate inflation
Yearly plan	5 years	14 working days	£20 a month	£200 a month	fixed for 5 years
NS Ordinary Account	1 calendar month	none, except for large amounts	£1	£10,000	fixed for 1987
TAXABLE BUT TAX NOT DEDUCTED AT SOURCE					
Income Bonds	1 year	3 months [1]	£2,000	£100,000	variable
Indexed income bonds 1st issue	10 years	3 months [1]	£5,000	£100,000	depends on rate of inflation
Deposit Bonds	1 year	3 months [1]	£100	£100,000	variable
NS Investment account	1 month	1 month	£5	£100,000	variable

[1]: Interest on cash withdrawn in first year is halved.

National Savings deposit bonds: these are a lump sum investment designed to produce growth rather than income. The minimum initial investment is £100. This earns interest (currently at a before-tax rate of 12.25 per cent a year, though the rate can change), but rather than being paid out to you, the interest is added to your investment on the anniversary of your purchase. You can withdraw a minimum of £50 by giving three months' notice. If you withdraw during the first year, you only get half the rate of interest on the amount repaid.

National Savings yearly plan: this regular savings scheme has a guaranteed return. You make monthly payments of between £20 and £200 a month by standing order, for the first year, after which you are issued with a 'yearly plan certificate'. Interest is then added to the amount built up for a further four years. To get the maximum rate of return (which is currently equivalent to 8.84 per cent a year) you have to keep the money in the plan for the full five years. You can cash the certificate in early, but if you do so during the first year you get no interest. Your repayment is normally put in the post within 14 working days of your application being received. You can, of course, keep your money invested for more than five years, earning the general extension rate.

tax

The return from National Savings Certificates, Index-linked National Savings Certificates, Yearly Plan, and the first £70 of interest from an Ordinary Account, is completely tax-free. The return from all other National Savings investments is taxable, but is paid out to you without any tax being deducted.

pros and cons

The safety of National Savings investments makes them a useful part of a portfolio, and some offer an attractive interest rate. The tax-free investments are particularly attractive to higher taxpayers and people who are losing age allowance. Even the taxable investments are worth considering, especially for non-taxpayers, because they are among the few investments that are paid out before tax is deducted. The income bonds have the advantage of giving a monthly income, and index-linked National Savings Certificates provide a good hedge against inflation. However, there are restrictions and possibly financial losses if you want to cash in some National Savings investments.

shares

You invest your money in one or more (preferably several) companies. The return you get is made up of two parts:

○ income in the form of dividends paid by the company
○ a capital gain when you sell (or loss, depending on whether the share price rises or falls).

There are a number of market places for people to buy and sell shares. The main one is the Stock Exchange. Around 2,700 companies have their shares 'listed' on the Stock Exchange. A novice should stick to these shares, which are generally in older, well-established companies.

You can buy through stockbrokers, banks or other investment advisers, who usually charge commission. Although there is no minimum investment, the costs of dealing mean that it's not generally worth investing less than £700 in one company's shares – and to reduce your risk of losing money, you should aim to build up a 'portfolio' of shares in five to ten companies.

There is nothing you can do if you lose money by picking the wrong share. But if a member of the Stock Exchange goes bankrupt, there is a compensation fund.

tax

Share dividends are paid after basic rate income tax has been deducted. People who should pay no tax, or less than the tax deducted, may be able to reclaim the tax; higher rate taxpayers will have to pay more. If you make a capital gain when you sell, there may be capital gains tax to pay.

pros and cons

Shares give you the possibility of making a capital gain to protect your investment against inflation. And if chosen correctly, the dividend can provide a regular, if fluctuating income. But only invest money you are prepared to lose, and be careful about cashing in your investment: do not necessarily do it on a pre-ordained date (such as, for example, the day you retire) because this may be a time when share prices are low. You should be prepared to leave your money invested for a long time, because of this fluctuation in price. Do not put all your money in shares, or invest in them if you cannot afford to buy shares in several companies. Instead, consider unit trusts, investment trusts, and British Government stocks as alternative investments.

single premium bonds

You invest your money with a life insurance company and the value of your investment is linked to one of several funds the company runs, such as property bonds, managed bonds (a mixture of property, shares, and fixed-income investments), equity bonds (shares), gilt bonds (British Government stocks), and so on.

With many companies you can, at low cost, switch your money from one fund to another.

Technically, the bond has a life insurance element, but this is very low. All it really amounts to is a return of your money if you die.

The bonds do not normally pay out an income as such, but you can get one by arranging to cash in part of your investment either from time to time or on a regular basis. As long as you do not cash in more than the equivalent of 5 per cent of your original investment, what you draw out is tax-free at the time.

You can usually sell your bond at once, or within a month. You will get a capital gain from the bond if the value of the fund in which it is invested rises. You could, of course, make a loss instead.

The minimum investment varies with the company, but can be from £500 upwards.

tax

If you choose, you can cash up to 5 per cent of your original investment each year without paying tax at the time, although you may have to pay income tax when you finally cash in the bond (if you are a higher-rate taxpayer). Gains when you cash the bond are free of capital gains tax, and of basic rate income tax, but if you are a higher rate taxpayer there may be higher rate tax to pay.

pros and cons

There is no income; you get capital gain, which you can cash in. Like unit trusts and investment trusts, single premium bonds offer a convenient way to invest in places which would be too risky for a private investor to invest in directly. There is the possibility of making a capital gain to guard against inflation, but there is a possibility of making a loss instead. For this reason these bonds should be regarded as a long term investment for money you are unlikely to need at short notice (when prices may be low). The life insurance company makes an initial charge and annual management charge.

unit trusts

This is a way of investing in the shares of UK and foreign companies, and, sometimes, British Government stocks. You buy units in a trust fund which invests in many companies (so if one company does badly, you lose only some of your money). The shares' performance is reflected in the price of the units, which can go up or down.

Your return comes in the form of:

o income paid in the form of 'distributions', made up from dividends from the shares the unit trust invests in; you can usually choose to have the income reinvested in more units rather than paid out

o a capital gain (or loss, depending on whether the prices of your units rise or fall). The success of your investments depends on when you buy and sell.

Some unit trusts concentrate on providing a high income, others on providing a high growth; you can choose which type – income or growth – suits your needs better. You can also choose between general trusts, which invest in a wide spread of companies, and trusts which specialise in investing in another country or area of the world, for example, the USA, the Far East, and so on. Roughly speaking, the more specialist funds are more risky than general funds, but can produce the highest growth.

You buy direct quite simply (no need for a broker) through coupons in newspaper advertisements, for example, or by post. Unit trust companies make an initial and an annual management charge. The minimum investment is generally between £250 and £1,000. Some unit trust companies also run regular savings schemes, usually with a minimum monthly investment of around £50.

tax

Income from a unit trust is paid after basic rate income tax has been deducted. People who should pay no tax, or less tax than has been deducted, can claim tax back; higher rate taxpayers will have to pay more income tax. You may have to pay capital gains tax on any capital gain.

pros and cons

Because of the possibility of making a capital gain, unit trusts can protect your money against inflation. It is also a convenient way of investing abroad if that appeals to you. But since you could lose your money, only invest in them money you can afford to lose, and don't invest just in one unit trust. Be prepared to treat them as a long-term investment.

how investments are taxed

investment	liable for income tax?	has basic rate income tax (or its equivalent) already been deducted from income?	any higher rate income tax to pay?	liable for capital gains tax?
annuities	yes – on the part which is interest	yes, normally	yes	no
bank investments	yes	yes, and non-taxpayers cannot claim tax back	yes – on grossed-up income	no
British Government stocks	yes	normally yes, but not if bought through National Savings Stock Register	yes	no
building society investments	yes	yes, and non-taxpayers cannot claim tax back	yes – on grossed-up income	no
income bonds	yes	depends on way bond works – ask company	depends on way bond works – ask company	no – but company pays tax on gains
local authority stocks and yearling bonds	yes	yes	yes	yes
local authority loans	yes	yes, and non-taxpayers cannot claim tax back	yes – on grossed-up income	no

National Savings bank	yes – but not first £70 of interest on Ordinary Account	no	yes	no
National Savings certificates and Yearly Plan	no	no	no	no
National Savings Deposit shares	yes	no	yes	no
National Savings Income Bonds	yes	not as such, but no more basic rate tax to pay	yes	yes
regular-premium life insurance savings schemes	no	no – but no basic rate tax to pay (company pays tax)	no – unless policy cashed in during first 10 years or three-quarters of term if less	no – but company pays tax on gains
single-premium bonds	yes – may have to pay higher rate tax when finally cashing the bond	no – but no basic rate tax to pay (fund pays tax)	yes – when you finally cash bond	no – but fund pays tax on gain
unit trusts	yes	not as such but no more basic rate tax to pay	yes	yes

INDEX

some other Consumer Publications

Wills and probate
is a layman's guide to making your will without employing a solicitor and how to administer the estate of someone who has died. For making a will, it tells you how to assess your likely estate, what to consider when appointing executors and a guardian for children. It shows you how to ensure that your will is free from ambiguity: what to say and how to say it, so that your wishes can be carried out without complication, how a will should be signed and witnessed and what to do when you wish to alter your will. It explains the implications of inheritance tax and capital gains tax and points out where and how tax can be saved.

For someone called upon to act as an executor, the probate section of the book is a step-by-step guide through the procedure, including sections on calculating the assets, how to get and fill in the probate forms, carrying out valuations, dealing with the bank and what to do while the accounts of the deceased are frozen, paying inheritance tax and dealing with income tax and capital gains tax, and all the other tasks that need to be performed in order to get a grant of probate. After probate has been granted, the executor has to deal with transferring property, selling or transferring shares, encashing national savings, gathering in the assets and distributing the legacies and bequests to beneficiaries.

The book also explains what happens, and what has to be done, if there is no will and the next of kin have to cope with the administration.

What to do when someone dies
is a companion volume to *Wills and probate*. It aims to help those who have never had to deal with the arrangements that must be made after a death – getting a doctor's certificate and registering the death, deciding whether to bury or cremate, choosing an undertaker and a coffin, selecting the form of service, claiming national insurance benefits. It explains the function of people with whom they will come in contact, often for the first time: the

doctor, the registrar, the undertaker, the clergyman, the cemetery or crematorium officials and, in some circumstances, the police and the coroner. The executor or nearest relative has to make the decisions, often at a time of personal distress; the book describes what needs to be done, when, and how to set about it.

No attempt is made to deal with the personal or social aspects of death, such as the psychology of grief and shock, the rituals and conventions of mourning, or attitudes to death.

Earning money at home

for anyone who wants or needs to take up an activity at home that will bring some extra (or essential) cash, this book sets out what is entailed. It puts forward the pros and cons of working at home, stressing the self-discipline required and the reorganisation that may be necessary. The statutory requirements about planning permission, liability for insurance, national insurance and tax are all explained. Advertising and getting work, costing and charging for it, getting supplies, keeping accounts, are all important factors that are fully covered. The second section of the book suggests some types of work that might be suitable, with or without previous experience, giving a brief account of what may be involved in undertaking them. Courses for brushing up a skill or hobby to a more professional standard are suggested, and sources of further help and advice are given. The final section discusses, optimistically, how to expand the business when successful.

Starting your own business

for people who have the courage, imagination and stamina to try a new venture on their own, this is a competent guide to help them through the essential steps. It advises on defining precisely what product or skill you have to offer, how to raise the necessary capital and cope with legal requirements. It deals with all the financial aspects: pricing the product, calculating overheads and cash flow, keeping accounts and other records, dealing with taxes including VAT, marketing and selling, premises and insurance. Throughout, sources of advice and information are given to help the small businessman make a success of going it alone.

The legal side of buying a house
for buying an owner-occupied house in England or Wales, this book will guide you step by step through the legal procedure. It explains what is involved and follows in detail the whole process of doing your own conveyancing – from placing a deposit, obtaining all the relevant forms and filling them in, dealing with the Land Registry and local authority, to exchange of contracts and, finally, completion. Even if you have decided that doing your own conveyancing would be too time-consuming or difficult for you, this book will help you check what your solicitor is doing at each stage. The book also deals with the legally less complicated procedure of selling your house.

Living with stress
helps the reader to cope with the many and various stresses in life, including the stress of loneliness, sickness, bereavement. It points to the more common warning signs and indicates what can be done to adapt where nothing can be changed.

Renting and letting
is a book which helps to clarify the legal position of all who pay rent to occupy their home, and anyone who wants to let property. The law of landlord and tenant is complex and confers rights as well as responsibilities on both sides. The security of a tenant's home, both in the private and the public sector, is safeguarded by law, but a prudent landlord need not be discouraged from letting, provided he fully understands the legal implications. The book explains when a landlord cannot get vacant possession from a tenant, and in what circumstances he can. It includes sections on rent control and getting a fair rent registered, explains the meaning of protected and statutory tenancy and what happens on the death of the original tenant. It deals with the repair obligation of landlords and the various protections a tenant has, including protection from harrassment and eviction and explains the council tenant's rights, including the right to buy the rented property.

Which? way to buy, sell and move house
takes you through all the stages of moving to another home –
considering the pros and cons of different places, house hunting,
viewing, having a survey, making an offer, getting a mortgage,
completing the purchase, selling the present home. It explains
the legal procedures and the likely costs. Buying and selling at an
auction and in Scotland are specifically dealt with. The practical
arrangements for the move and for any repairs or improvements
to the new house are described. Advice is given for easing the
tasks of sorting, packing and moving possessions, people and
pets, with a removal firm or by doing it yourself, and for making
the day of the move go smoothly.

Divorce – legal procedures and financial facts
explains the procedure for an undefended divorce and deals with
the financial facts to be faced when a marriage ends in divorce.
Aspects covered include getting legal advice, conciliation, legal
aid and its drawbacks, the various financial and property orders
the court can make, what can happen to the matrimonial home,
the children, how to calculate needs and resources, the effect of
tax, coping with shortage of money after a divorce. Each couple
faces different problems: the book illustrates the effects of alternative financial solutions to various personal situations on divorce.

What to do after an accident
helps you to know what to do if you are injured or your property
badly damaged by someone, who you can claim on and for what.
It explains your legal rights when another person's negligence
has caused you harm and how to set about claiming compensation and recovering after an accident on the road (as driver,
passenger, pedestrian, cyclist); at work (employers' liability,
state benefits); at home (as visitor or occupier, when burgled); out
and about (in a shop, on public premises, in the street, by an
animal or a child). It provides guidance on court proceedings,
negotiating through lawyers, making insurance claims (on your
own or another's policy), applying for statutory payments,
assessing damages, medical treatment, coping with disability,
getting back to work.

Understanding cancer
explains the nature and causes of the disease most people find more frightening than any other. It tells you how to recognise some of the symptoms and avoid some of the risks, and explains how cancer is diagnosed. It goes into the details of various forms of treatment: surgery, radiotherapy, chemotherapy, including their possible side effects, and takes an objective look at the role of alternative/complementary therapies. It describes some of the advances in cancer research but does not pretend that these will soon provide the long awaited cure. The book deals with advanced cancer and terminal care but stresses that cancer must not be regarded as inevitably fatal.

Children, parents and the law
describes the legal responsibilities and rights of a parent, and of a child towards parents, so far as they exist. It deals with illegitimacy, when things go wrong in the family, with education, if a child comes up against the law, when a child has to go into the care of the local authority, and explains what is involved in custodianship, guardianship, adoption, fostering. It sets out at what ages a child can carry out specific activities – from buying a pet to getting married. There is a section explaining the effects of a child being injured and of the death of one or both parents.

Consumer Publications are available from Consumers' Association, Castlemead, Gascoyne Way, Hertford SG14 1LH, and from booksellers.